# No Nation for Women

T0024530

*For Sita*
*my mother, the force of nature*

# No Nation for Women

## Priyanka Dubey

**SIMON &
SCHUSTER**

London · New York · Sydney · Toronto · New Delhi

A CBS COMPANY

First published in India by Simon & Schuster India, 2018
A CBS company

Copyright © Priyanka Dubey, 2018

This edition published in 2018

The right of Priyanka Dubey to be identified as author of this work has been asserted by her in accordance with Section 57 of the Copyright Act, 1957.

1 3 5 7 9 10 8 6 4 2

Simon & Schuster India
818, Indraprakash Building,
21, Barakhamba Road,
New Delhi 110001

www.simonandschuster.co.in

HB ISBN: 978-93-86797-08-7
PB ISBN: 978-93-86797-09-4
eBook ISBN: 978-93-86797-11-7

Typeset in India by SÜRYA, New Delhi

Printed and bound in India by Replika Press Pvt. Ltd.

Simon & Schuster India is committed to sourcing paper that is
made from wood grown in sustainable forests and
support the Forest Stewardship Council, the leading
international forest certification organisation.
Our books displaying the FSC logo are
printed on FSC certified paper.

No part of this publication may be reproduced, transmitted or stored in a retrieval system, in any form or by any means, electronic, mechanical, photocopying, recording or otherwise, without the prior permission of the publisher.

This book is sold subject to the condition that it shall not, by way of trade or otherwise, be lent, resold, hired out, or otherwise circulated, without the publisher's prior consent, in any form of binding or cover other than that in which it is published.

# Contents

*Introduction*                                                         vii
*Author's Note*                                                        xi

1. 'Corrective' Rapes of Bundelkhand                                    1

2. Tripura: The political nature of rape/sexual crimes                 15

3. Story of Sexual Crimes against De-notified                          28
   Tribes of India

4. Rapes in Small Towns and Rural India                                41

5. In the Dark: In custody rapes                                       59

6. The Anatomy of a Rape in Haryana:                                   79
   The Bhagana gang-rape case

7. On Sale—Trafficking Girls:                                         105
   Story of four tribal girls divided by geography
   but united by fate

8. Hanging from a Mango Tree:                                         124
   The rape and murder of the Badaun sisters

9. Sexual Abuse and Rape of Children:                                 152
   'What are we doing to our children?'

10. Rape As a Tool for Establishing Caste Supremacy                   164

11. Rape and Sexism Inside the Indian Police Force            180

12. Rape in West Bengal: The land of regimental             201
    politics

13. The Question of Rehabilitation of Rape                  218
    Survivors in India: Policy and ground realities

*References*                                                236
*Acknowledgements*                                          239

# Introduction

THE SEED OF THIS BOOK WAS SOWN IN MY CHILDHOOD AND IS enmeshed in my upbringing and formative years. I grew up in a conservative family in a far-from-glitzy town in North India. As a child I struggled to understand my place in the world, the position that women occupied in our society.

Later, as I trained and learnt as a reporter over the years, I found myself particularly drawn towards reportage on issues around gender, social justice and violence. Then the 2012 December gang-rape happened in Delhi. Here I want to mention that I have spent most of my reporting career working for magazines and writing long-form articles. As a result, I had to read books, research papers and other reference material related to the subjects that I was working on. Since most of my reporting was circling around gender and social justice for years, I started looking for books on rapes in India to improve my own understanding of the subject. To my surprise I was not able to find much on the subject. There were a couple of edited anthologies and books on violence against women that took place during the India–Pakistan partition—but I could not get my hands on a reportage based non-fiction book that would help me understand the problem of sexual violence in India. That was when I realized that this was an urgent book waiting to be written.

I have always strongly believed that India is a diverse country and you cannot put your finger on any one story and turn it into a sweeping generalized statement about the whole country. Gender crimes against women also have multiple dimensions and facets here. Patriarchy is the nucleus of this problem and all other factors contributing to violence against women manifest themselves around it.

The chapters written in this book attempt to document one slice and one dimension of each of the many aspects of rape and violence against women in India. From this humble and very limited attempt, I hope to present a true and comprehensive picture of the problem of rape and violence against women in India.

I have been a reporter all my life and I have utmost faith in the power of a true report. I have exercised my training as a reporter while verifying facts and to ensure that all aspects of every story find voice in these pages.

The original draft of this book had 15 chapters. After a lot of brainstorming with my editors we decided to drop two chapters. One of these was on the 1991 Kunan Poshpora rape case and the other one was on India's self-claimed godman Asaram—recently convicted for raping a minor girl.

During the course of finishing the reporting and the writing of this book a large number of published articles had already been made available in the public domain on the above two cases. Hence, we decided to leave out the stories that had been told in the recent past or by the survivors themselves.

India has seen an unprecedented 873 per cent rise in crime against women in the past five decades. The figures are only growing with every passing year. The most recent figures given by the National Crimes Records Bureau (NCRB) of India says that 106 women are raped in India every day. Four out of every 10 of these victims are minor girls. This means more than four girls are raped every hour in the country. This is essentially saying that in less than every 15 minutes, one woman is raped somewhere in India.

While there is no authentic research to establish that this increase in numbers showing the crime against women graph going up every year is primarily because more women are reporting rape—the fact that speaking up against sexual abuse still remains a stigma needs no confirmation. Most women opt out of reporting sexual crimes because of the 'victim-shaming' attitude prevalent in India.

My own journeys across the country have taught me that the roots of this victim-shaming lies in patriarchy. The imposed concept of body purity for women turns into a monster of unbearable shame and stigma in the case of sexual assault. All these concepts of so-called honour, 'body purity' and 'body pollution' have been created and nourished for centuries by this very patriarchal mindset.

Chapter by chapter, different aspects of this deep-seated patriarchy is placed in front of the readers—along with the narratives of women and their families who are fighting centuries-old prejudices. In the process, the reportage also lays bare the nexus of state, caste, religion and politics that works together to support patriarchal biases.

It took me six years, to collect and write these 13 stories. During all these years, I worked mostly on shoe-string budgets, depending heavily on general human goodness and the kindness that friends as well as strangers showered upon me. Sometimes by driving me on their motorbikes in the hinterlands, sometimes by insisting that I spend the night in their homes and sometimes by offering me a meal of *dal-chawal* to eat in the middle of a forest. In that way I see this book as a collective effort of all the people who have helped me in my journey in many big and small ways.

Now as this work is almost ready to see the light of day I feel like a mutant of my old self. Years have passed by. I kept rewinding and listening to the interview tapes sitting in my cheap, rented accommodation in Delhi. Each reporting trip, each recorded voice and each chapter altered something inside me. I kept slipping in and out of the darkness of my own self.

I am full of gratitude towards this book—working on it provided me with a protective refuge for my own vulnerable self.

My time with the women and their families—whom I met during the six years of my numerous journeys—gave me courage, confidence and infused immeasurable amounts of compassion in me, which kept me going throughout. I am most grateful to all the women who shared their stories with me. While voicing their stories, I found my own voice.

I hope these chapters add to our collective understanding of the crisis of rape in India. Acknowledging and understanding are the first steps towards fighting sexual crimes against women.

PRIYANKA DUBEY

# Author's Note

THE NAMES OF ALL VICTIMS—ALIVE OR DEAD—HAVE BEEN changed in this book to protect their identities. Also, names of immediate relatives and family members of the victims have been changed for the same reason. In compliance with Indian law, the exact locations of the victims' residences have also been altered.

This is a work of nonfiction entirely based on the author's first hand reporting experience of more than six years across India—except for some of the southern states—which could not be covered due to monetary and time constraints.

The chapters written in this book are backed by extensive ground research, field travels to the remote corners of the country and interview tapes of hundreds of people running into hours. The list also includes important documents, including copies of multiple court cases, public interests litigations, first information reports, post-mortem reports, paper clippings, transcripts and different human rights reports. Every fact mentioned in this book has been cross-checked and vetted.

Initial reporting on some stories—reportage that later became a part of this book—was first published by different media publications.

The author acknowledges direct or indirect contributions of all her editors for encouraging and supporting public interest journalism. She thanks everyone who has been a part of this journey for the same.

# 1

# 'Corrective' Rapes of Bundelkhand

BUNDELKHAND. HERE IS LAND, PARCHED, BROWN.

Stretching across large swathes of Madhya Pradesh—districts such as Damoh, Orai, Banda and Chhatarpur—and parts of Uttar Pradesh, Bundelkhand's vastness gets reemphasized by its desolation. Trees wither here. The soil is hostile.

Bundelkhand is also no woman's land.

~

In 2009, as a student of journalism, I lived in Bhopal—a city that is roughly 350 kilometres from Bundelkhand. Mornings were devoted to attending classes; afternoons were marked by idyllic scooter rides; and evenings were meant for plays at Bharat Bhavan.

It was only in April 2011, while working as a correspondent for a national magazine, that I was alerted to the crisis in my 'backyard'—through a small single-column news item in a regional Hindi daily, with a title that (when translated) read: 'Eighteen-year-old girl burnt alive after rape in Chhatarpur, Madhya Pradesh'.

The report offered vague outlines of a tragedy, little else.

I felt compelled to trail the story. As I began scouring for information, I learnt of a two-year-long pattern of extreme violence in Bundelkhand's arid wilderness. Teenage girls, who happened to reject the advances of men, were routinely raped, then brutally killed. Some had their kerosene-soaked bodies burnt; others were hanged; still others, who managed to get away and approach a police station, were caught, then killed.

This was 'corrective' rape and murder. This was a land telling its girls that there were lethal consequences to saying 'no' to men.

I would go on to document 15 such victims over the course of my investigations; all of them had lost their lives between 2009 and 2010. Yet their stories had been systematically pushed away from the line of vision of the nation. For the mainstream media, these women did not exist.

≈

In the summer of 2011, I began my inquiries into the spate of corrective rapes in Chhatarpur.

The town has no station—and I was constrained by a shoestring reporting budget—so, I decided to catch a train to Jhansi and then an early morning bus to my destination.

Tatkal ticket in hand, I found myself in the sleeper coach of the Bhopal Express for the first leg of my journey. Even as I compiled a list of exploratory questions in the lower berth of my compartment, a group of boys, jubilant after having appeared for a recruitment exam for the Uttar Pradesh police force, entered my coach. A couple of them groped me, some hovered close, many passed lewd remarks—this went on till I disembarked at Jhansi.

It was post-midnight. I was trembling. The railway police could not be found. There was a women's waiting room—it was deserted—and there, I spent the next four hours, huddled in a corner, till I could catch the local bus. As I waited, I thought about the harassment I had been subjected to in the train compartment—and I compared my own helplessness to that of the victims I was about to document. Could I tell the dead girls' families that I understood their offspring's trauma; that even while playing the role of a reporter decrying patriarchy, I was a victim of a chauvinistic system? Could I tell them that they could trust me with their stories because my narrative was a part of theirs?

Or was it tactless of me to make such proclamations. After all, I had emerged relatively unscathed, while the women in my stories had been raped and killed?

At the break of dawn, I caught a state bus, and reached Chhatarpur district. I had a list of questions for my subjects; I had a list of questions for myself.

~

That April, I travelled a distance of around 130 kilometres from the Chhatarpur district headquarters to Batiagharh near Damoh. The route to Batiagharh is dotted with sparse plantations of teak; the soil is dry. Batiagharh knows drought and penury.

In this remote town, I traced my way to 35-year-old Phoolbai's residence. The wooden door of her one-room mud hut was closed to keep out the scorching afternoon sun. The verandah was plastered with yellow mud. Beyond, scantily clad children, their faces layered with dust, aimlessly walked through the derelict neighbourhood.

Phoolbai took her time to open the door. Dressed in a yellow and red printed sari, she stood before me, her eyes sore. The inner walls of her house were painted dark blue. Two small children, aged three and five, sat quietly on the mud floor, surrounded by clothes and utensils. Phoolbai's husband Munno Adivasi, in his mid-40s, was at work—he was a daily wage labourer.

Even before I could ask my first question, Phoolbai started sobbing; she pointed towards a corner of her house: '*Yahain jalaya tha use. Mitti ka tel daalkar jala diya maari modi ko ba ne.*' (He burned her right here. He poured kerosene on my daughter and burnt her alive right here.) When I followed the direction of her finger, I saw blurred grey marks—layers of ash—testimony to her child's suffering.

Phoolbai's 14-year-old daughter Kalabai was allegedly murdered on 20 March 2010 inside her hut. 'It was the month of Chait (the first month of the Hindu calendar, corresponding to March),' Phoolbai recounted. 'It was a Monday. The time was around five in the evening. I was working in the field when a young boy from our neighbourhood came running towards me. He was screaming: "Your daughter has been burnt alive, Kalabai has been burnt alive!" Kalabai's father and I immediately started running towards our home. We found our daughter on the mud floor of our verandah, her body burning; she was still alive. She was screaming, crying, gasping, thrashing about.'

Phoolbai told me that she fainted for a few seconds. 'I was shocked. But then, I took hold of my emotions and placed my daughter on my lap. My husband rushed to the sarpanch. The whole village gathered in our verandah. But nobody moved; everyone simply watched as my daughter yelled—it was as though she were an object on display. Finally, my husband and the sarpanch arrived at our doorstep, and it was in the latter's vehicle that we went to the hospital in Damoh.'

Kalabai had suffered 95 per cent burn injuries.

Approximately 24 hours later, while Phoolbai held her hand, Kalabai passed away.

A year after Kalabai's death, Phoolbai revealed to me that her daughter had announced, before all who had gathered, the name of the offender. 'That boy—my daughter's murderer—I don't know why, but he had been stalking her for a while. Never did we think that he would do something this dastardly,' Phoolbai said.

'My daughter, in her statement to doctors, revealed the events of that awful day. While I was working in the fields, she said, the boy forcefully entered our house. He raped her. Since she resisted all through, he was livid. He found a full can of kerosene in our kitchen and doused my daughter with it. Then he flung a burning matchstick in her direction. He ran away. *Modi saari jal gayi maari, maari modi jal gayi.* (My daughter was burnt alive, my daughter was burnt alive.)'

The accused was arrested three months after a case was filed by the parents at the Batiagharh police station; in April 2011, when I interviewed Phoolbai, the trial was yet to begin.

At the Batiagharh police station, the cops would only disclose the sections under which the case had been filed. When I persisted with my questions—why was the progress so slow; what was delaying justice?—the only officer in the police station shifted responsibility. 'The victim's family comes under the scheduled tribes,' he said, 'so the case has been registered under the SCST (Scheduled Castes and Scheduled Tribes) Act. In our area, only *bade sahebs* (key officers) look into SCST cases. I cannot help you any further.' He shrugged indifferently.

Phoolbai informed me that the cops did not visit her house—not for questioning, not for investigating the crime scene. She claimed that they had not received a copy of the dying declaration of their daughter, or even a copy of the First Information Report (FIR). Phoolbai and her husband do not know the name of their government lawyer; they barely know if there is a lawyer pursuing the case.

Wiping her face with the corner of the pallu of her sari, Phoolbai told me, 'We do not know what is happening. In any case, how can we pursue this matter? Kalabai's father is usually out all day. I am in the fields. If we stop working, how will we feed the two children who live? Sometimes, I believe that the accused will be released from jail; his family is powerful, hails from a high caste, and has money. They know everyone in town.'

Phoolbai stood up and placed a *peetal ka paraat* (a deep dish made of brass) in front of me. Summoning all her willpower, she whispered, 'I had saved money and bought this brass container for my daughter's wedding.'

Then, as though provoked by that memory, she said, 'My husband and I—we will work overtime. We will take loans. We will do whatever we can. But we will fight the case to the finish in court. I am not going to die till my daughter's killer is punished.'

～

The Hama village panchayat of Chhatarpur district is just seven kilometres from the district headquarters. On a regular summer afternoon, one spots men with large white cotton scarves or gamchas wound around their faces, walking down a pebbly route, past rows of houses and hillocks. There's rarely a woman to be seen.

If I visited Hama, it was to talk to Kantadevi Richariya. I waited in her one-room hut, plastered with brightly coloured prints of Hindu gods. Soon, I spotted her—vivid, in a printed black-blue sari and white cotton blouse—striding down a lane speckled with broken red bricks. She balanced a firewood bundle on her head. As she entered the porch of her house, she kept the firewood in the verandah, wiped the sweat trickling down her forehead with her pallu, then entered the doorway.

When she saw me, her eyes welled up with tears. Within seconds, she was howling. I held her hands in mine, my eyes moist. We hadn't spoken a word, yet I could sense the enormity of her sorrow.

Gradually, Kantadevi started talking. 'It all happened on 4 March 2010. That afternoon, Rohini's father and I were working in the fields. When we finished the day's work, we started making our way back home. We were at the periphery of our village when our neighbour Meena-badhai came running towards us. She shouted that our daughter Rohini had been burnt alive.'

Phoolbai's narrative repeated itself here—as Kantadevi rushed home, found her 18-year-old daughter Rohini in agony, and heard her yell the names of the offenders. Then, Rohini gasped, '*Mummy paani pila do.*' (Mummy, please give me water.) Soon, she died.

I learnt that Rohini, who used to keep home while her parents worked, had attracted the attention of a family in the vicinity; they wanted Rohini to marry their son. Kantadevi recalled, 'Five months before my daughter's demise, the family started coercing us—this, despite the fact that we had offered our daughter's hand to someone in Alipura. Rohini's father ended up having a squabble with the family patriarch on the matter. His son believed that our refusal was an insult to his caste, clan and family.

'The boy had been stalking Rohini. And when we refused his parents' demands, he—and three other boys related to him—found Rohini in our verandah while we were at work. They raped her. As she resisted, they made her sit on a stool'—Kantadevi pointed to a wooden stool in her verandah—'and burnt her.'

Kantadevi claimed that Rohini had named all four accused in her dying declaration, and had signed against the statement. Yet, the defence lawyer of the accused successfully proved in court that the declaration—the central piece of evidence around which the case was built—was invalid. He asserted that the absence of 'a note on the physical and mental status of the victim while giving the dying declaration' was a major loophole. In his view, the victim, with 100 per cent burn injuries, was mentally unfit—in a state of 'delirium'—and her version of the truth could not be trusted.

This is the only 'corrective rape' case I know of where the lower court has passed its judgment. On 18 January 2011, the judge—after citing major discrepancies in police investigations, in a 28-page-long judgment order—gave the benefit of doubt to three of the accused and signed their release orders; the fourth happened to be on the run.

For Kantadevi, the nightmare did not end with the judgment. Her family was boycotted by the village. '*Gawn wale kehte hain, ham par hatya lag gayi hai.* (The village people say that the murder is our fault.) What can I say? The police, lawyers—everyone—they're powerful Rajputs. Earlier, we were under immense pressure to withdraw the case and now, after the acquittal, we keep receiving threats. Our children are not secure.

'I don't understand this. Those who killed my daughter are free, while we, as grieving family members, are shunned.'

~

I met Devilal Patel on a blazing afternoon in April 2011, in Mugdhapura, Nohata tehsil, Damoh, roughly 200 kilometres from the Chhatarpur district headquarters.

Seven months before our meeting, Devilal Patel had been a cheerful farmer in his mid-40s, strolling the mud streets of Mugdhapura with a smile on his face, waving out to neighbours. When I met him, his gait was slow; his eyes drooped and carried dark circles; and he hid in the shadows of his house, trying to escape the gaze of his locality. His feet, cracked along the soles, peeped out of torn black slippers. His lips were blood-red, chapped. His wrinkled off-white shirt and cotton gamcha were damp with sweat.

Like Kantadevi and Phoolbai, Devilal wept. Like them, he barely recognized his life after the brutal murder of his daughter.

Kamyani had been all of 17. She had been one among a handful girls from Mugdhapura who had made it to high school. Devilal—committed to making his only daughter stand on her two feet—used to personally send her to teachers seven kilometres from his house. His belief was that with a solid education, his daughter would escape the shackles of a social order that had restricted him.

Yet, on 19 October 2010, Devilal's dreams for his girl shattered. It all started the preceding day—on the afternoon of 18 October 2010—when Mugdhapura was bringing in a religious festival. Schools were closed, and most parents were attending a local puja. A listless Kamyani decided to take a walk at five in the evening. Even as she ambled down the deserted fields, a resident of her village allegedly raped her. It was Kamyani's brother who heard her cries for help, and as he approached her, the assaulter ran away.

Devilal recalled his daughter's anguish. 'She was in pain.

We took her to the nearest police station at Tejgarh. It was around eight at night. The police questioned her for the next six hours; my daughter kept crying. I don't know if they filed an FIR, but I remember it was the middle of the night when I brought my girl home.'

News that father and daughter had approached a police station spread like wildfire. The next day, Devilal claimed, five men from his village, including the rape-accused, burnt Kamyani alive. Her 'crime' was that she had 'dared' to file a complaint at the local police station against a man who had raped her the previous night.

To her last breath, Kamyani fought; despite sustaining 95 per cent burn injuries, she mustered the will to give a statement to the police in front of hospital doctors, and sign her dying declaration.

Forty-five days after Kamyani's death, the local police arrested four of the five accused. Yet, by the time I visited Devilal, three of them were out on bail, and one was on the run. Devilal lowered his head as he spoke: 'The whole village is urging me to compromise and give up the fight for justice. The accused men come from a powerful family. They're landlords, while we are poor farmers.'

When I visited the Tejgarh police station, the staff was clueless about the case; when I persisted with my questions, I was shown a copy of the FIR but there was no information on the investigations being conducted. Later, in a seedy chamber in Damoh's district court premises, the public prosecutor fighting Kamyani's case told me that the matter was still pending in court. Then, he shrugged, 'Generally, in such cases, witnesses turn hostile due to the lure of money and muscle pressure.'

Back at Devilal's home, I met his wife, Nirmala. 'I

can never forget my daughter,' she said, then produced a photograph. 'See! How beautiful my child was! May nobody else suffer this misfortune—of seeing a child die in a mother's lap. My daughter turned to ashes before me.'

Then, Nirmala produced another photograph—of herself next to her daughter, both standing tall, shoulder to shoulder. Nirmala's head was covered with her firozi sari's pallu; her daughter Kamyani was in blue jeans and a black shirt. 'We always believed that she was a different child,' Nirmala said. 'And then, she died.'

~

Roughly nine centuries ago, Delhi's only woman ruler Razia Sultan was at the cusp of greatness. Minhaj al-Siraj, a noted historian of that era, wrote in his magnum opus, *Tabaqat-i-Nasiri*: 'Razia possessed all the qualities of a ruler. She was more capable than her brothers. But she had one weakness. She was a woman.' Thus, she was murdered.

More than 900 years have passed, but Minhaj's words still resonate in the barren plains of Bundelkhand.

During the course of investigations, I spoke to a number of local policemen, lawyers, doctors, politicians and local activists to identify why 'corrective rapes' had become an unchanging, unchangeable pattern in parts of Madhya Pradesh. A number of reasons were cited—among them the region's extreme backwardness. A senior police officer, who had worked in Bundelkhand for over two decades, told me, 'The fact that Chhatarpur still does not have a direct train line tells you something—Bundelkhand is impoverished. A feudal order prevails, and there's no hope for industrialization or employment. Crime, then, is the only avenue for escape.'

Now, imagine a region that is not just economically

backward, but also largely patriarchal—where power hungry, ungainfully employed men are propped up by a false sense of machismo. In such a region, women become the immediate targets of criminal activity. The chief public prosecutor of Damoh, Rakesh Shukla, told me, 'Out here, an upper caste man's fragile sense of self gets threatened if a girl dares defy him; he *must* retaliate! And he does.'

In this land, dominated by men, women are rendered powerless. During a late night interview, Aruna Mohan Rao, inspector general of police (crime against women), told me, 'Policemen do not take complaints from women seriously. We are trying to sensitize our police forces but it's going to take time.'

Worse, even if a woman (or her family) were to file a complaint, systemic problems assert themselves. When I asked Rakesh Shukla how the accused in Bundelkhand managed to get bail and evade conviction, he admitted: 'Policemen may fail to prepare a foolproof FIR, may delay the process of filing a charge-sheet—as a result of which the accused have sufficient time to secure anticipatory bail—or may not capture circumstantial evidence and leave loopholes in the investigative process. Then, there are doctors who may not prepare medical reports; witnesses who may turn hostile; and defence lawyers who likely will highlight contradictions in all statements, so the accused are given the "benefit of doubt". And all this could happen because the accused belongs to an influential upper caste family, or is affiliated with one.'

It could also happen because, out here, women, no matter how victimized, are held culpable for men's crimes of omission and commission. I recall a meeting with a senior police officer in Damoh. It was early dusk, and the police station's porch had been freshly plastered with cow dung. There was no electricity, and all the constables ogled as I interviewed their boss, the town inspector, and took notes by candlelight. On the condition of absolute anonymity, the inspector said, 'The fact is, most of our girls burn themselves of their own accord, and die. Earlier, women were known to be patient; they would attend to household chores and live quietly within their homes. These days, girls have no forbearance. *Zara kisi ne halka kuch kaha nahi ki gusse me khud ko aag laga letin hain! Arre, aurton ko to samundar ki tarah sehansheel hona chahiye, ye sab to hota hi rehta hai.* (They get angry at the slightest provocation and burn themselves! They should be patient like the ocean. Everyday vexations are normal.)'

With this being the dominant outlook, the schemes initiated by the Madhya Pradesh government—among them 'women's empowerment' and '*beti bachao, beti padhao*' (save the daughter, teach the daughter)—have received a lukewarm response at best. Ashok Das, the chief home secretary of Madhya Pradesh at the time of being interviewed, assured me that every attempt would be made to address the epidemic of 'corrective rapes' in Bundelkhand. He swore to create special 'sensational and heinous crimes' cells; to fast track cases of sexual violence against women in courts; to set up a committee comprising a district superintendent of police, a district judge and district collectors to address the rape crisis; and to get the chief minister to personally monitor its progress every three months.

Broken promises, all.

≈

As I board a rickety bus from the Chhatarpur bus stand, and head to Bhopal, dusk gathers. Bundelkhand is a place of shadows.

It's a long journey. I have time to think of the families I have met; to re-imagine Kalabai, Kamyani and Rohini; to distract myself with copies of FIRs, and birth and death certificates.

The horizon is an ominous black. I leave Bundelkhand. But Bundelkhand's girls never leave me.

# 2

# Tripura

## The political nature of rape/sexual crimes

IT'S THE FIRST WEEK OF JULY IN 2016 AND ROUGHLY 2500
kilometres away from Delhi, I am standing at the north-
eastern tipping point of the country: Tripura. The sky in
Tripura's capital city, Agartala, is cloudy this morning.

I take the national highway 44 from Agartala and start
moving towards Khowai district which falls in the western
part of the state. After driving for around 45 kilometres, we
reach the main market of Teliamura town.

Situated on national highway 8, Teliamura is a sleepy tribal
town. With the Bangladesh border running parallel a few
kilometres away, I am truly at the north-eastern end of India.

Though it was raining throughout our drive from Agartala,
a wan sun has now popped up above the sky of Teliamura. A
few locals are selling betel nuts on both sides of the highway.
It's late afternoon and I am waiting for someone here.

After a couple of minutes, I see 50-year-old Meenakshi
walking towards me. Dressed in traditional Hrangkhawl tribe
attire—the local tribe to which she belonged—she walked
towards me and we shook hands. Her handshake had the

confidence of a person comfortable in public spaces. After all, she was a local politician and a contestant in local village level elections. More on this later.

The first thing I noticed about her was that one of her eyes was injured. She had a swollen bump-like structure all around that wounded eye. She had stuffed a betel nut inside one of her cheeks which she kept chewing on all afternoon. She was wearing a purple pawnzel—a skirt-like lower garment worn by Hrangkhawl women. Above it, she wore a plain deep red loose blouse and had covered her head with a red checkered *gamcha*. I remember, she was smiling since the minute she met me and I can never forget that sparkle in her eyes.

She lived in the neighbouring Budhrai Para village which was more than three kilometres away from the main Teliamura market. There was no concrete approach road to her village and it could be reached only on foot. We started walking towards her village. She was leading the way through picturesque postcard-like serene paddy fields. I was following her, mesmerized by the landscape. Numerous small ponds were interspersed in the rice fields and I remember crossing a small stream too. The fields were surrounded by dotted lines of trees which would intensify and convert into small forest-like patches in between.

As we reached Meenakshi's village, I figured that residential huts were not situated in clusters like in North India. Every house was on its own, surrounded by its own palm trees, its own small ponds and fields. Meenakshi's nearest neighbours lived at least 600 metres away on a separate hillock-like structure. The entire village was populated by Hrangkhawl tribals, a sub-tribe of the Malsom Tribe, native to Tripura.

Meenakshi's house was surrounded by large palm trees. A fishing net was lying in front of the main door of her two-room house. There was a pond and children's clothes were drying on a wire by the bank of the pond.

Her village comes under the Tripura Tribal Areas (TTA) Autonomous District Council (ADC) which is an independent council administering the *Tripuri*-dominated areas of Tripura. Here the term *'Tripuri'* refers to the 'original inhabitants' of Tripura.

At that moment, while removing my mud-laden shoes outside Meenakshi's house, I remember feeling a deep sense of overwhelming gratitude. For being able to reach till this point of the country, the land of the 'original inhabitants' of what is now known as the old *historical twipra kingdom*. This was unlike any other part of India that I had travelled to before.

Like the rest of Tripura, the ADC has also been politically dominated by the left parties here. After being a loyal member of the Communist Party of India (Marxist) (CPI-M) for years, Meenakshi decided to leave the left cadre in late 2014. She then joined the Bhartiya Janta Party (BJP) and went on to contest the ADC village council elections held in 2015.

Meenakshi's very clean house was almost empty—except for a clothes stand and a basic old bed. A young girl from her family was making tea in a small kitchen located in one corner of the room. The youngest of her three children, her 19-year-old son, was standing next to us. We settled down on plastic chairs that were brought from a neighbour's house.

'Rapes happen due to all kinds of reasons in India. But here, in Tripura, women are raped due to political witch hunting,' is the first thing that Meenakshi says as soon as we start the interview.

I look at her face as she nods and continues with conviction, 'I was raped by a CPI(M) cadre man because I dared to leave the left and join the BJP.' She went on, 'It happened in March this year (2016). The date was 24th. It was dark and around seven in the evening. I was on my way back home then, walking from the Teliamura market towards my village. I have lived here all my life so normally I am never afraid while walking around. So I was walking back as usual with a torch in my hand. Just then I felt that someone is walking behind me. Before I could understand, he grabbed me from behind. I recognized him immediately. He was Dumpa Hrangkhal, the 26-year-old son of a local left leader. He grabbed me and forced me on the ground. Then he hit me on my forehead with the torch. He started beating me with that torch and he raped me. I fell unconscious.'

We are both aware of the presence of Meenakshi's youngest son in the room. I look at him for a second and see him quietly wiping his tears.

Meenakshi goes on, 'My husband died long ago. I have three children... all of them are grown up, adults now. I am an old woman. At this age, one becomes carefree. You do not imagine a sexual attack on yourself at this age. But he did not only rape me, he actually tried to kill me. There was blood all over my upper body. I lost one of my eyes in that attack and now I have partial vision. That night, after beating me he covered my body with grass to hide his deeds from passers-by. He was sure that I am dead. But by god's grace, I survived.'

The matter took a political turn after news of Meenakshi's rape got published in the local media. She does believe that she was attacked because she changed her political allegiance. 'Here in villages, the left cadre men are more powerful than in cities like Agartala. They do not allow people to vote for any other party. We had been voting and working for the left for so many years but our situation did not improve at all. Only the families of local left leaders are getting richer. So I decided to try BJP one time. That's my right as a citizen—to try another party if the first one is not working enough for the welfare of the people. I contested in the 2015 ADC village council elections. BJP gave me a ticket from my village and I fought against the left. The local left leaders were after me ever since then. They used to pass remarks and threaten me to withdraw. I lost the election but I fought and never withdrew on the face of threats. They hated my guts and my choice of representing any other party in the village. During election campaigning, the accused had said he will teach me a lesson and put me in "my place" one day. I ignored but a couple of months later, he did what he had claimed.'

After the village sarpanch (headman) refused to interfere in the case citing it as a 'political matter between two parties', a criminal case was registered against the accused at Teliamura police station. Meenakshi's medical examination confirmed rape.

The accused surrendered after three months of sustained police effort to find him. But Meenakshi feels that the police did not investigate her case properly. 'They were under the influence of the state government. One month after the incident, my son and his friends saw the accused in a forest nearby our village and we immediately informed the police. But the officers there said "how can they locate a boy in a forest?" They did not even bother to come and visit us once. It was only after big BJP leaders from Agartala came down here to Teliamura and spoke to the cops that they started taking this seriously.'

Currently the accused is under arrest and the case is up for trial. Meenakshi adds, 'It's a nightmare... living with the memories of that night is a nightmare. Sometimes I wake up suddenly in the middle of the night and find myself sweating.

I am not able to walk around freely in the village anymore. All the time I feel someone is coming from behind and is going to attack me. I have developed a habit of walking with my head turning back to check who is walking behind me every five minutes. I feel like my head turns around at the slightest sound while walking. I feel scared all the time. That is why I am looking forward to the trial beginning as soon as possible. Because along with justice for myself, I also want closure.'

After the news of a 'political rape' started making rounds in the local press, official spokespersons of the Tripura unit of CPI(M) condemned the attack on Meenakshi and said that they have no association with the accused.

By the end of our conversation, Meenakshi's son has moved around the room. He is now standing behind her, holding her chair. After gently keeping his hands on his mother's shoulders he says, 'Ma will fight the next election also from whichever party she wants to fight. I will be with her all the time now.' Meenakshi looks up at her son and her face breaks into a quiet smile. 'My eldest son works as a football coach in Agartala, the second one works in Bangalore. This is my youngest. He now lives with me and shadows me wherever I go. After the incident, all of us have become cautious. But come what may, I am not going to let anything deter my spirits. I will fight the next village council elections as well. All I want is to improve mine and my village's situation.'

~

My next stop was Shikarbari village situated in the Tulashikhar block of the West Tripura district of the state. Since Shikarbari falls in a predominantly tribal part of Tripura, I requested a local reporter friend—well-versed with the language and area—to accompany me to this village.

As we embarked on our 72 kilometres long journey from Agartala to Shikarbari, the first 'brief' my journalist friend gave me was about how politically sensitive this part of India was.

'The Bangladesh border runs parallel to this village Shikarbari. It's one of India's last border villages. If you had arrived just seven–eight years ago, you could have been abducted by insurgent groups from the main market road of Tulashikhar. Just like that! And no one would have been able to find you—it's that sensitive. This whole belt has a history of tribal insurgency and the area around Shikarbari was specially a militant stronghold.'

I had previously read about how the insurgency issue in Tripura was resolved by the mid-2000s, but I had no clue about the specific situation of Tulashikhar.

By the time we reached Shikarbari, it was around one in the afternoon. It was a particularly humid day and we were here to meet the family of 27-year-old Preetamma. In February 2010 she was gang-raped, murdered and then left hanging from a wooden pole near her village. This all happened just 11 days before she was scheduled to contest ADC village council elections. Three Tripura State Rifles (TSR) jawans have been charge-sheeted in this case.

We walk through roughly one kilometre of rice fields and a pond to reach Preetamma's village. Her mud house is one of the first houses in the village. Her father, who is in his late 70s, starts crying as soon as her name is mentioned. 'She was my bravest child, but she went away too early,' he says while settling down on the mud verandah of his house for a conversation.

The family told me that Preetamma was married with two children but she left her husband's house and came to

Shikarbari to live with her parents around five years before her death. She complained of domestic violence and never went back to her husband. Her two children lived with her and their maternal grandparents in the village.

Tears do not stop flowing from Preetamma's father's eyes throughout our conversation. 'After the separation from her husband, she had become very socially conscious... in a good way I mean. She wanted to make things better for the people of this village. She wanted a better future for her own children. That is why she had decided to contest local elections. She was getting threats after filing her nomination papers. We were all a bit nervous... but we had never imagined that it will go this far,' he said.

Preetamma mother joined in at this point. Preetamma's youngest child was in her lap when she walked in. Sending the child away to play, she sat down with me for a conversation. 'It was the night of 19 February 2010. My daughter had filed the nomination papers and voting was to take place in around 10 days' time. She was in between her preparations for the elections. We were all a bit sacred but we thought if she wins... she might change the poor circumstances of our family and this village. But that night she took out time to attend a neighbourhood wedding. On her way back, she was gagged by some drunken TSR soldiers. They raped her at the house of a local left party supporter. Then they murdered her and tried to hang her body from a wooden pole in the forest outside our village to make it look like a suicide. But some other villagers saw them doing this. But by then my daughter was dead.'

I am told that the village used to have a local TSR outpost at the time of the incident. 'The outpost was created because militancy was strong at that time,' a villager told me. That outpost has been removed after this incident took place.

Preetamma had filed her nomination papers on a NCT (National Conference of Tripura) ticket, a local regional party. In an official statement given to the media after her murder, the then national sectary of NCT, Animesh Debbarma had blamed the local CPI(M) cadre for their candidate's brutal end. 'She told me that some local left members were trying to threaten her and were forcing her to withdraw her nomination papers. That is why we were concerned about her safety. She was careful about her movements until the last date of withdrawal of nomination papers passed. But it could not prevent her gang-rape and murder in the end.'

Though the accused were from TSR, the incident took place in the house of a local left volunteer. Under heavy criticism from the opposition and media, the then chief minister of the state, CPI(M)'s Manik Sarkar, condemned the attack and recommended a higher level investigation by CBI (Central Bureau of Investigation), India's premier investigative agency.

The CBI later charge-sheeted three TSR soldiers, namely Dipak Tripura, Ananta Hari and Narayan Ghosh for the gang-rape and murder of Preetamma. After six years, the trial is still dragging on in Khowai District Court.

The victim's father is still crying.

The wrinkles hanging on his deep brown face are now all wet with tears. It was a heart-breaking sight. He kept gazing at the mud wall in front for a few minutes and then slowly said, 'My daughter was ambitious. We were all sure that she was going to win the election. That is why they killed her right before voting was to take place. Later Manik Sarkar came to our house. He was sitting here with me where are you are sitting right now. He promised me that his government will keep both my grandchildren—my deceased daughter's son and daughter—in state government hostels and will facilitate their education. He promised me that he will educate my grandchildren. So many years have passed by; my grandchildren are still here. Nothing happened.'

Preetamma's daughter is now nine years old while her son is six. Children know about the court case and the story behind their mother's death. The daughter being older has clear memories of her mother. Her grandmother tells me that she still sometimes wakes up in the night and cries for her mother.

Looking at his grandson playing in the verandah, the victim's father adds, 'After waiting for government help for years, we have now put them in our local government school. We neither have the strength nor the money to raise these kids. I am poor and old now. I and their grandmother—we can die any day. What will happen to Preetamma's children after we are dead?'

∼

The conversations with Preetamma's parents and Meenakshi are ringing in my ears. How and why did political rapes became a pattern in Tripura?

With an abysmally low conviction rate of 24 per cent in cases of sexual crimes against women, the National Crime Records Bureau's 2015 figures portray a grim picture of Tripura. According to official government figures, the rate of crime against women in Tripura is 68.2 per cent, which is much higher than the national average of 54 per cent.

Back in the state capital Agartala, I meet women rights' lawyer Kalyani Roy to understand the issue more comprehensively. Kalyani has been taking up cases of violence against women in the state for more than a decade now. On a Sunday morning, I reach her residence located in a Bengali neighbourhood of Agartala. She finished her morning pooja and fixed breakfast for her husband and kids before sitting down for an interview in her residential 'office room'.

She started by saying that women don't have proper political representation in the state. 'See, Tripura has been ruled by the left for more than two decades now. Their cadre is everywhere and there is little tolerance towards candidates of other parties. Especially if those candidates are women. Now women's participation in politics in encouraged here. But ONLY as a faceless crowd. Only as space fillers. The moment they attempt to fight elections, they have to face backlash.'

~

Roma Ghosh, a woman in her mid-30s, endorses Kalyani's opinion but names BJP as an equally intolerant party when it comes to women. I met Roma at another human rights lawyer's office in Agartala. After a neighbourhood argument escalated, she was tied to a pole in a temple in Agartala, beaten and molested publically in 2014. 'The accused made a video and uploaded it on YouTube. The whole world saw how my clothes were torn and how I was beaten up. My case is still going on in court. Me, my husband and my children—we were trying to find a way of dealing with the unprecedented media attention that my family was receiving after the video of my abuse went viral. We were all shattered. Then leaders from the local BJP women's wing came to my house and made promises of bringing me into politics. They took me to a press conference and gave interviews to the media from my side. After using me to target the incumbent who then left the government, they vanished from the scene. I got no help from anyone. I feel my wounds were exploited by local BJP women leaders.'

~

Apart from the overall political apathy, Kalyani also adds that crime against women is rising in Tripura at an alarming rate. 'Now every day at least five to six women come to me for consultation. Most of them opt out of filing an FIR because there is just no institutional support for them. The whole system is crumbling.'

During our 90 minutes long interview, Kalyani spoke at length about the issues that are plaguing the judicial process for rape survivors in the state. She said, 'Where should I start? There are no active functional traces of the 2012 rape victim compensation scheme in this state. Even medical superintendents in government hospitals are not aware that rape victims are entitled to free, immediate and priority-based medical care. We don't have any forensic lab in the state. The police are especially lax when it comes to investigating and collecting evidence in a rape case. In rural areas, there is intense pressure on victims to compromise. And the police's behaviour is also discouraging; victims opt out of filing an FIR. And the whole story stops at this point.'

Before leaving Tripura, I met a couple of other civil society activists from Agartala. Most of them did not wish to be named. But their thoughts reiterated Kalyani's. One recurrent narrative in all these conversations was 'the apathy of Delhi-centric media'. A human rights activist I spoke to, expressed surprise on my reporting visit to the state and said, 'It's true that politically motivated rapes have happened in Tripura. All political parties along with the administration are responsible for failing the women of this state. But what do you have to do with all this? You are coming from Delhi, aren't you? We in the Northeast—especially us living in Tripura—we don't exist for you. The central government is not bothered about us. Similarly for you, we are people living on the fringes of India. Our lives don't matter to all of you.'

I believe it's important to document here that there is anger and a strong sentiment of feeling neglected in the intelligentsia of Tripura. Which is understandable. But it's also important to mention that I got a lot of support and encouragement from locals while collecting the reportage for this chapter.

It's just that they hope to see more reporting from the Northeast on a regular basis in mainstream national 'Indian' newspapers.

# 3

# Story of Sexual Crimes against
# De-notified Tribes of India

## 'Time Heals'

This, I suppose, is one of the world's most given truisms. When your loved one dies or when love dies, someone around you will come and say 'time heals'.

Well, truly, time does heal most things—except perhaps when there is a denial of suffering and injustice. While growing up, I remember reading in a library book: 'There is no bigger violence and injustice in the world than to NOT acknowledge suffering of victims of violence.' Can time ever heal the wounds of a person whose suffering is denied?

The story of the 11 Pardhi women of the Betul district of Madhya Pradesh is a living example of how time cannot heal everything.

It's also a story of how the de-notified tribal groups in India have been historically and collectively wronged for generations. Forget justice, even acknowledgement of the occurrence of grave sexual crimes against women is a distant dream for the Pardhi community of this tribal district.

In September 2007, a settlement of 350 Pardhis, a minority nomadic tribal community living in the Multai tehsil of Betul, was razed to the ground by a group of local hooligans. Eighty-five houses were burned down, two Pardhis were allegedly murdered, while 11 Pardhi women were allegedly gang-raped. All this happened in the presence of all major senior district administration officials and an array of local politicians representing all political parties active in the area.

Local police worked on the case for two years and then the matter was transferred to the CBI. But, nothing except a few arrests have happened in the last decade of the matter dragging and languishing in different local and high court benches of Madhya Pradesh.

Most surprisingly, after repeated questioning and repeated deposition of statements, not even an FIR was ever registered on the complaint of 10 Pardhi women who said that they were gang-raped on the night of 10 September—just before their huts and shanties were burned down. However, charges were framed in the case of the gang-rape of the 11th woman—who was also one among the two members of the community who was allegedly murdered.

## Who are Pardhis?

But before taking you through this complex story of racial violence, rape and murder against the Pardhis of Betul and stressing on how this is an important part of the narrative of endemic violence against women in India, let's start with the basics. Who are Pardhis? And how did they end up at the bottom of the growth ladder of the Indian social fabric?

Well, the answer to this question goes back to the colonial era when India was ruled by the British. Or perhaps even before—in the Mughal era.

The word 'Pardhi' originates from the Marathi word *pardh* which means 'hunter'. Pardhis are part of the 60 million people who make the 'Denotified and Nomadic Tribes' (DNT) of India. Historically associated with a nomadic life, excellent knowledge of forests, wildlife and unmatched hunting skills, Pardhis now live in small pockets in the states of Maharashtra and Madhya Pradesh.

According to a folklore popular among the Pardhi community, their ancestors are said to have supported King Maharana Pratap in his wars against the Mughals. After their king's defeat, the Pardhis pledged to never settle down at one place. So they kept moving from one forest to another, surviving mostly on their hunting skills and vast knowledge of the wild flora and fauna.

Later, when the Pardhis resisted the British occupation of India, the then British government ruling India listed them under what they called 'criminal tribes'.

In 1871, the British government brought in a new act called 'the Criminal Tribes Act of 1871' and slotted around 150 Indian tribes under this act, which according to the British had 'criminal tendencies'. This gave the then British police wide powers to arrest, control and monitor the movements of the tribes listed under this act. After independence, the Indian government withdrew the Criminal Tribes Act and brought a new law called 'Habitual Offenders Act, 1952' in its place. Till date, most nomadic Indian tribes, including the Pardhis, are controlled by this act.

Just like its predecessor, the Habitual Offenders Act is equally regressive and negates the fundamental principle of the Indian judicial system—innocent until proven guilty. Multiple debates are going on in the Indian Parliament and court rooms demanding absolute invalidation of this racial and discriminatory law which tags a section of Indian citizens as criminals from birth.

Pardhis, who are listed as a 'denotified nomadic tribe' under the Habitual Offenders Act, are classified as scheduled tribes in most districts of their habitation. Like the rest of India, Betul also has a history of racism and violation of tribal rights. Being tagged as a 'born criminal' under this act, the Pardhis of Betul have always been a soft target to blame for any wrongdoing or crime that happens in the area.

## The Pardhis of Betul

The story of the 2007 rape, murder and arson of the Betul Pardhi settlement was also the result of a similar prejudice—of seeing Pardhis as criminals. But how did the nomadic Pardhis start living in Betul in the first place?

Betul is a tribal district with more than 40 per cent tribal population. And Pardhis have always been living in the forests of Betul and the adjacent Amravati district of Maharashtra. Conversations about rehabilitating Pardhis and other nomadic tribes have been going on since forever in the Parliament. In one such effort, in 1996, the Pardhis of Betul were given 11 land plots on the outskirts of the Chauthia village of Multai tehsil of the district. Distributed for their permanent settlement, under the Indira Gram Awaas Yojna, these 11 families were also given additional financial help to build their houses on these plots. Slowly, other Pardhis of Betul joined them and the Chauthia village settlement came to be known as *Pardhidhana*.

Fifteen years after the Pardhis settled down in Pardhidhana of Betul and four years after they were uprooted from their homes, in October 2011 I made my first reporting trip to

Betul. The month was almost ending and a nip had already entered the breeze. I took a train from the state's capital Bhopal, passed through the picturesque Satpura hills and a stretch of thick timber and teak forests to reach this small sleepy town in the heart of central India.

A few kilometres away from the railway station, the Pardhis of Chauthia village were living in polythene tents built on an open ground situated in the heart of this small town. Secured with sewed patches of cloth rags and jute bags, the condition of these tents was deplorable. But for the roughly 350 Pardhis living in these tents, life was going on. The open tents and the polythene bathrooms that appeared like shadows of the tents did not pain them. Hunger, lack of food and fear of creeping reptiles did not bother them. Incessant rainfall, bone-chilling winters and the scorching summers of central India were stitched into their DNA; it seemed that they took it all in their stride. What pained them though was the non-acknowledgement of the ongoing racial discrimination that they have been facing for years. Even with empty stomachs, the thought of justice was what brought tears to their eyes.

They gathered all around me as soon as I reached their open tents. And the first thing they told me was that they want justice and dignity in accordance with the Constitution of India.

They want their piece of land, their lost homes, their piece of sky and their share of human dignity.

~

Now, back to Betul in September 2007.

The cycle of violence here in the Chauthia village began from 9 September 2007. Early morning, on this day, the body of a raped and murdered woman from the Kunbi caste was found in a neighbouring village. Local residents were immediately convinced that the 'criminal' Pardhis living in Chauthia village's Pardhidhana are behind this crime.

Rumours spread like wildfire across the area and anger against the local Pardhis started shimmering. It was decided that the 'Pardhis with criminal tendencies' should be dragged out of the region. Soon local politicians like Raja Pawar and Sukhdev Panse stepped in to encash on the situation. Pawar was then a zila panchayat member from BJP while Panse was an elected MLA from Congress. Video recorded evidence of them provoking locals, inciting them to raze the Pardhi settlement to the ground and ensuring them the administration's support for all this have been submitted in courts.

Meanwhile, the local police rounded up all members of the Pardhi community as 'suspects' in connection to the rape and murder that took place in the neighbouring Sandiya village. The Pardhis told me that 'they were all forced in police vans like animals and taken to the Multai police station'.

Later, police zeroed in on two Pardhi men—residents of Amravati district of Maharashtra, next to Betul. Pardhi men from the Chauthia village helped the police in catching the two murder suspects from Amravati. Named Dharmraj and Bhoora, these two suspects were caught the same day by Betul police. But this did not calm down the residents of Chauthia.

After spending hours at the Multai police station, the residents of Pardhidhana came back to their homes by the afternoon of 10 September. But, in less than a couple of hours they were asked to vacate their homes and move away immediately.

Alsiya Pardhi, who is leading the struggle of Chauthia's Pardhi community, says, 'We had heard rumors that locals were planning to burn our houses so we did not want to leave that day. But the police told us that our lives were in danger. They asked us to reach Bhopal and stay there for a couple of days till matters cool down in our village. SDOP sahib himself assured me that he will take care of our houses. I had never imagined that he will stand as a mute spectator while our houses will be razed down.'

By late evening the Pardhis of Chauthia village were again rounded up by the police, hoarded in police jeeps and then dropped at the Multai railway station. From here, most Pardhis took buses and changed trains to reach Bhopal the next morning. Twenty-five-year-old Kapoori Pardhi told me that they were not allowed to pack anything. 'The cops came and started thrusting us in police vans. I couldn't understand what wrong we have done? Why were we being forced out of our own homes? On top of that, they did not allow us even five minutes to take whatever little cash or any jewellery or valuables that we had. We left our homes penniless like beggars. I think that is why we are living like beggars till now.' As she speaks, Kapoori keeps on staring at the soil beneath her feet.

Everyone went away but 10 Pardhi women who were held back by the police. I asked myself why.

≈

I remember we were all sitting in the Utkrisht School ground in Betul. Roughly 70 polythene Pardhi tents were situated all around, mostly empty as all the residents were sitting around me. It was post noon and the sun was beating down above our heads.

While talking about their forced exodus from their homes, some Pardhis started shouting, some stood up and enacted how the locals were all hell-bent on uprooting the 'criminal'

Pardhis from their homes, one old woman started howling while others were staring at the land on which they stood or scratching their bodies.

When I ask about the 10 Pardhi women held back in the Pardhidhana on the night of 10 September, a silence suddenly falls over the crowd.

I am told that six out of the 10 women are present and I can talk to them separately. The rest have gone begging in town. Next I walk away with these six women. We look for a place to sit and settle down on a patch of dry land behind the last row of tents. There is a sewage drain flowing in front of us and all of us are sweating because of the afternoon heat.

The women tell me that they were gang-raped that night by a group of men, which included local residents, cops and local politicians. They tell me that they have complained at multiple police stations from Bhopal to Betul, they have given detailed statements to people from the National Commission of De-notified and Nomadic Tribes (NCDNT), local police and later also to the CBI about the incident but nothing happened.

While talking to me, one of them looks up at the sky while another stares at the ground. Others keep moving their hand to keep flies at bay. I look at them as they talk—they were all beautiful women with deep big eyes. When I think of them now, I can imagine them peacefully walking in the woods, walking miles and miles and crossing one forest after another like their ancestors. I can see them plucking fruits and looking up at the morning sun with gratitude in their eyes. With the help of my readings and little anecdotal knowledge that I have acquired while working on the Pardhis, I imagine these women 10 years younger. I can see spirited women with hope in their eyes, and a cheerfulness which has been the symbol of the forest lives of the Pardhis since centuries. Today these women, with their beautiful sad eyes are just a shadow of their own past.

As they talk, I can't stop thinking about the generosity of their spirit. The fact that they walked away from their nomadic lives with an open heart to embrace the modern world with a free spirit, but got only sexual violence, racial discrimination and the tag of being a 'criminal tribe' in return, reminds me of the situation of marginalized communities throughout our modern world.

The oldest among the six, Woman A starts talking first. She shows me scars of the wounds around her lower ribs and back. 'Four years have passed by. But even now whenever my husband finds some money to buy cheap roadside alcohol, he gets drunk. And then he gets angry and screams. He says that I was gang-raped and then beats me. I know that he can't do anything to those who raped us that night. But he feels terribly angry for me. The easiest thing for him on such nights is to beat me. So he abuses and beats me.'

A must be in her late 30s but deep wrinkles have already started showing up on her face. She looks at me with stone-like blank eyes and keeps scratching her scalp in between the conversation.

S takes over from A. She didn't remember her age but appeared to be in her mid-30s and came across as most fearless among all of them. She looked directly into my eyes and said, 'We were stopped by SDOP Sakalle that night. Our husbands and all others from the Pardhidhana were being dispatched to the railway station by the police. But Sakalle asked us to stay back and said that he will get us dropped in his vehicle, safely. Since he was from the police, we trusted him and obeyed. But around the time when it started getting dark and all of our people went away, we started worrying. I remember it was eight o'clock by then. When we went up to the officer and asked him to send us to our husbands, children and other family members, he started laughing. There were other men with him there. We have named Jagdeesh, Vijaydhar, Sanjay Yadav, Ashok Kevde and others in our complaints. When all of them started laughing, we couldn't understand what was happening. Then one of them said, '*Sandiyan wali bai ke saath jo hua, ab wahi tum sab ke saath hoga* (Whatever happened to the woman in neighbouring Sandiya village, will now happen to you).'

The women told me that S's house was the biggest pucca house in Pardhidhana. The women were raped in different rooms of this house. Suddenly the three-year-old daughter of B crawled towards us. She was howling.

Taking the child in her lap B added, 'Before we could make sense of what was going on, they were dragging us to the rooms. There were around three to four men in each room. *Poora saadi lugga sab faad diye the didi* (They tore our clothes and raped us). We kept pleading and begging them to leave us but they wouldn't listen. Our clothes were all torn and we had nothing to wear. Later we all wore S's saris, somehow covered our bodies and ran towards the railway station.'

It was a harrowing night for these 10 women. They had no money to buy train tickets. They changed trains and stood in front of coach toilets to avoid ticket checkers. By morning they somehow reached Bhopal and were united with their families who were camping at Bhopal's railway station. But the ordeal of the Pardhis of Betul was just starting.

Next morning in Betul, people from around 10 neighbouring villages started gathering around Chauthia village. At 8 am the crowd was of roughly 400 people. By

10 am it swelled to 2000. Local journalists Akeel Ahemad and
Reshu Naidu who have submitted video recorded evidence in
the matter to CBI and different courts met me in Betul. They
showed me the raw footage of the morning of 11 September
2007. Reshu says, 'I saw hordes of people gathering around the
Pardhidhana. They came on tractors, cycles and motorcycles.
The mob started burning the huts of the Pardhis and breaking
down the numbered pucca houses in the *mohalla*. Politician
Raja Pawar himself climbed up on a JCB to ensure that the
house of Alsiya Pardhi was broken.' Nodding in agreement
Akeel adds, 'Huts of Pardhis were burning down and fire
brigade vans were standing silent on the other side of the
road. Policemen were mute spectators. Mob was razing down
the settlement and slogans like "*In apradhi Pardhiyon ko Betul
se khaded dena hai*" (We have to drag these criminal Pardhis
out of Betul) were being raised. Politicians were provoking
the mob. People broke and burned down houses. And every
physical thing which could be looted from the Pardhi basti
was looted and taken away.'

Next day, on 12 September 2007, dead bodies of two
Pardhis, a man and a woman, were recovered one kilometre
away from the Pardhidhana. This woman was the 11th
woman who was raped on the intervening night of 10 and
11 September in Pardhidhana. And she, along with the other
man who was killed that night with her, were the parents of
Langdu and Ram Pyari.

In their late teens, Langdu and Ram Pyari both live in one
of the polythene tents in the Utkarsh school ground in Betul.

That night, Langdu and Ram Pyari were returning to
Pardhidhana after grazing their goats the whole day. Their
parents and nine other Pardhi villagers were with them. As
they came near Pardhidhana, they heard loud noises and saw

fumes coming up from their houses. An eye witness named Saudageer Pardhi told me that all 13 of them were scared on seeing the chaos going on in Pardhidhana.

'We could see fire and hear loud noises. And we could sense that something is wrong in our village tola. So we decided to halt one kilometre before our village. We hid ourselves behind trees. But by then some locals spotted Langdu and Ram Pyari's parents. They ran towards us. I remember they were shouting, "*Aaj ek bhi Pardhi ko nahi chodenge*" (We will not leave a single Pardhi today).'

When I meet Ram Pyari and Langdu for the first time in their makeshift tent made of yellow tarpaulin, they stare back at me with blank eyes. After 10 minutes of silence, Ram Pyari looks at me with a stony face and says, 'There are 11 eye witnesses to the rape of my mother and murder of both my parents. This includes me and my brother. Nothing has happened till now. We have spoken to everyone from the CBI to the police to judge sahib. Nothing happened. What do you want to know? Nobody can understand my helplessness.'

Her voice chokes and eyes well up. Again a spell of silence descends on all of us.

Later, after we resume our conversation, the children narrate a bone-chilling account of how their father was stoned to death by the local mob, led by small time local politicians. 'First they hit my father with stones. He fell down. Then they did the same with my mother. We were all scared so we kept hiding behind trees at a short distance. Then I saw men grabbing my mother and raping her. Around 10 men took turns on her. All of us saw. Then they picked her body and threw her in a nearby well,' Landgu told me, wiping the tears flowing down his cheek. After the mob went away, the children ran to check on their parents. Their father had bled to death. Their mother had drowned in the well.

A three-member commission of the NCDNT visited Betul a couple of days after the Pardhis were pushed out of their homes in Pardhidhana.

In their report, the commission stated that 16 houses and 69 huts of the Pardhis were destroyed rendering around 350 Pardhis homeless. The commission made a strong recommendation of registering cases in the matter of the alleged rape of 11 Pardhi women and murder of a Pardhi couple. Also, the commission asked for a quick investigation from the police and rehabilitation of the Pardhis from the district administration.

While cases have been filed in the matter of the two murders and destruction of the Pardhi settlement, not even an FIR has yet been filed in the case of rape allegations made by the 10 Pardhi women.

As the sun sets over the Betul sky, S breaks into a satirical grin. 'Just because we are Pardhi adivasis, there is no justice for us. If you would have registered our cases, investigated and the court would have decided that we are lying—we would have somehow made our peace with the fact that we lost our case in court. But you are not giving us a hearing! When I am saying that I was raped by three men, when I am saying this again and again in front of 100 police officers, the CBI *wallahs,* the court people—I am saying again and again—why are you all not listening to me? Years and years have passed by and not an FIR has been registered. All because I am a Pardhi adivasi woman with no rights. What place do I have in this country?'

My stomach churns and I bite my lower lip to hold back the tears. This was one moment when my pen stopped taking notes.

Time Heals? Not always.

# 4

# Rapes in Small Towns and Rural India

**'I am only waiting for justice.'**

There are many remarkable things about the extraordinary story of 23-year-old rape survivor Neelam. But the one thing that has been etched in my memory is her voice. I first met her in June 2013 in her native village situated in the Bundelkhand region of Uttar Pradesh. She was a little older than 18 then. I still remember her voice and her subdued manner of speaking. She would make me sit close to her in her one-room mud hut, roll her eyes and look around to check on the eavesdropping security guard standing outside her house. And then speak in a low pitch voice as if sharing a secret with me.

Though the broader details of her 'story' have been published in local as well as national media, but newspaper spaces were always too cramped to house the entire story of a wounded soul. She had so much more to say, which she told me bit by bit during our hours' long conversation. Holding my hand at times and asking existentialist questions in between.

During December 2010, Neelam was raped by Indian politician Purushottam Naresh Dwivedi, who was then a

sitting MLA (member of legislative assembly) of the Bahujan
Samajwadi Party (BSP) from the Narani town of Banda
district. Neelam was a minor then who grew up in a scheduled
caste family in a Bundelkahnd village. She was the daughter of
a long time local BSP worker and being a sitting local MLA
from the same party, Dwivedi was 'worshiped' by her father.
After brutally raping her, Dwivedi also got her beaten up
gruesomely by his goons and then used his political influence
to put a false case of theft against Neelam in the local police
station.

After raping her, he also managed to get her imprisoned
in Banda jail for one month under fake theft charges. She
was released only after her story hit national headlines, when
things started to slip out of the local political control zone
of Dwivedi. After a five year long legal battle, and two years
after I met her for this interview, Dwivedi was found guilty
of raping her and was convicted by a Lucknow-based special
CBI court. He has since been sentenced to 10 years of rigorous
imprisonment.

But the story of what happened between these years and
her memory of the crime has not only changed the course of
Neelam's life but has altered her thought process at a deeper,
psychological level.

My journey of reaching Neelam started with contacting a
few local stringers based in the Banda district of Bundelkhand
where she lives. Most men in Banda I spoke to for putting
me in touch with Neelam, would first mock her as a
'temperamental woman', who has been 'speaking too much'
about the crime that happened to her. Some would break into
laughter, brimming with satire and dismiss her as an 'attention
seeking woman'. Cutting through the obvious patriarchy of
local media and residents, I contacted Neelam and she agreed
to meet me in her native village.

There are several laws to protect the identity of survivors in case of sexual violence in India. But Neelam's case is one of those rare cases which are known by the victim's name. Though we are not using her real name in this story she doesn't mind her name and other identifying details being used while writing about her elsewhere. Memories of a horrible crime and a bitter lonely legal battle pitched against a powerful elected local politician happening in Bundelkhand—one of India's most backward regions—has turned her into a person of many contradictions. She is very strong and brave. But she is also tired of being strong and brave.

I met her in the summers of 2013. She lives roughly 50 kilometres away from Banda railway station, in a village situated deep inside the agricultural fields of Naraini block.

On reaching her village I started looking for her house and got the same answer from everyone I asked. 'The hut which has five policemen standing outside is her residence.' It was not difficult to find her residence but I could already imagine the stress she would be feeling with a police troop guarding her house all the time. Police protection leads to a catch-22 situation for most rape survivors. In high profile cases where battles are pitched against men of power and influence, threats often follow and hence police protection becomes crucial for the safety of the survivor and her family. On the other hand, presence of a security troop alongside makes the survivor family easily identifiable and adds to the already mountainous challenges of facing the social stigma associated with rape.

As I entered her house, she was folding freshly washed clothes and listening to old Bollywood songs on her mobile phone. Dressed in a black track suit with her hair tied in a bun, she presented a contrasting portrait to the usual veiled women of rural Bundelkhand. She lives in a single room hut, a few metres away from her maternal house where her family—father and brothers—live together. There was a small fridge in her room, a small steel wardrobe and a wooden bed. There were utensils and clothes lying all around covering almost every inch of her one room hut. Her small verandah was painted by mud, a common practice in rural India. There was a small cot lying in the verandah which was used by the police protection team, including a woman constable, to sit on while on duty, guarding her house.

She started the conversation by complaining of headaches. 'That's why I am listening to music. It helps me in diverting my mind and reducing tension,' she said, switching off the music on her phone.

Neelam's mother passed away when she was a toddler. As a motherless child, she grew up extremely introverted, hopping between her father's village and her maternal grandmother's village situated nearby. She could not finish her school and remained an alienated child—curling into herself as she describes it—for most part of her adolescence years. She mentions that it has taken a lot of effort for her to make that journey from a shy girl to the outspoken warrior that she is today.

'I was never like this. As a child I was in the habit of hiding inside my house. I would not speak one word with any stranger. But what happened with me was so bad and torturous, that I had to change myself. I changed because that was the only way out for me. I had to speak up if I wanted to survive,' she said.

Neelam was 17 years and two months old when the crime happened. She recounts, 'My father was actively involved with the BSP for the past 17 years, which means almost since I was born. He used to manage the party affairs at the local panchayat level here in our village. As you know, Dwivedi was also an MLA from Naraini. Once he came to our village and paid us a visit. I was inside the house when my father asked me to bring a glass of water for the MLA. I went out and quietly gave him the glass of water. He took the glass from my hand and kept looking at me. He was actually staring at me and checking me out from top to toe. Then he started asking me random questions like where do I study, in which class, etc. I said I don't know as I did not wish to interact with him further. Then he turned to my father and said, "Your daughter is so beautiful and she does not speak much. Send her to me. We'll educate her, train her and get her married." My father agreed and said, "*Aap hi ki beti hai sahib* (She is just like your daughter)." In good will, my father even took me to his house once after that. But I refused to stay there. And since that day he was after my life.'

After Neelam refused to live at Dwivedi's residence, her father sent her back to her maternal grandmother's house. The family was struggling to make ends meet and poverty would often push Neelam's father to drop her at her maternal grandparents' house in a nearby village. But with her, poverty also only changed houses. It never actually left the family.

It was on one such December night in 2010, that she was kidnapped from her maternal grandmother's village. She recalls, 'I was asleep in front of my grandmother's hut when I was picked up. I remember they had tied my hands, my feet and my mouth with ropes and rags of cloth. The names of the men are Rajju Patel and Rajiv—both of them were MLA Dwivedi's men. They first took me to a nearby mahui jungle and held me captive there for three days. They kept me hungry and would torture me by thrusting my face in cold river water at night. While pushing me into the water they

would say things like how dare I turn down the MLA's offer?
After I was kidnapped, my father first lodged a complaint with
the local Naraini police station. He also went to Attara police
station which is near my grandmother's village. But his pleas to
the cops went unheard. Nobody would listen, no one would
pay any heed to his requests as he made the rounds of police
stations; weeping and pleading in front of police officers to
find his missing daughter. When he saw no hope from any
end, he turned to the MLA for help. Then the MLA started
working on his plan. He said, "*Ladki to ham chudhwa denge
par shart ye hai ki wo hamaare paas rahegi.* (I would get the
girl rescued but there is one condition—she will live in my
house after she's found)." He also told my father to not worry
about me as he will get me trained in livelihood earning skills
and then would get me married also. My father saw no option
but to agree to what the MLA was telling him. Soon after he
said yes, the kidnappers themselves brought me to the MLA's
house. It was 8 December 2010 when I was brought back to
my father. By now I was very sick, weak and was constantly
crying.'

Neelam breaks down into tears at this point. I give her a
glass of water which she drinks immediately. After a couple
of minutes she gathers herself and starts by expressing anger
on how Dwivedi first got her kidnapped and then made her
father agree to his demand of her living at the MLA's residence.
She adds, 'In front of my father he said, no more crying now.
Cook food here, work for us. We will train you in household
work, find a groom for you and get you married soon. Then
you will work for him as well as for us.' At that point of time,
neither father nor daughter understood what Dwivedi meant
by his 'work for him as well as for us' remark. They assumed
that Neelam would have to clean and cook at the MLA's house

and soon she would be married off. Her father was an old time ground worker for the BSP. He trusted Dwivedi's words and believed him.

In the intervening night of 9 and 10 December, Dwivedi walked into the room where Neelam was sleeping. 'I was tired after a long day's work and so I went to sleep. Suddenly he came in and removed the sheet I had wrapped around myself. Then he asked me if I remembered what he had told me the previous day. I stood frozen. He reminded me and said again that if I get married to the man he chooses for me, I will do "service" both for him and my husband. Then he shouted, "Didn't you understand what I'd said?" and asked me to remove my clothes. I started crying. I begged him and said, "Sahib, beat me as much as you want to beat me. Give me your shit to eat and I will eat it but please don't do this to me, sahib. I am your daughter,"' Neelam recalled.

Suddenly her voice dipped. She kept her hand on my hand lightly and went on, fighting back tears. 'My resistance enraged him. He turned away to fish for a blade as I kept crying. Then he slashed and tore all my clothes with the blade he had found. Then he began biting and scratching me like a beast. There were cuts on my face and my whole body was swollen. My feet were bloodied. He kept abusing me and then raped me. Also, he was continuously threatening me to stay quiet about this. He said he will shoot me point blank if I opened my mouth in front of anyone.'

The memories of the crime never left Neelam. Her body did not stop bleeding for several days. 'I cannot tell you didi, how much it pained when he raped me. He treated me worse than animals. I was so wounded that I thought I would die. No girl in my position would have been able to tolerate what I have survived. I was in so much pain that I was bed-ridden for weeks. I kept crying the whole of the next day but the bleeding wouldn't stop. There was no one I could have asked for help. I found a mobile phone and contacted my father. I told him to immediately take me away. He said he will come the next morning. But there was one more night for me to face before the sun would have come up again,' she adds.

The next night, Dwivedi again tried to attack Neelam. But this time she was alert, and managed to somehow slip away from the back door. But it was a cold December night in Banda and Neelam had no clue about the dark foggy world that stood outside the premises of Dwivedi's bungalow. She says the fog was so dense that night that she could not even locate the roads. But nevertheless, she ran for her life. And hid herself under the first bridge that she found on the road.

'I spent the night hiding in a drain along the nearby Turra Road. I was so scared, wounded and tired that the hours after this point are a blur. I remember burying my head in my knees and shivering out of fear and pain.'

The night somehow passed. Next morning, Dwivedi came looking for her. He had brought local cops with him.

Neelam told me that the MLA sent away the cops after she was found. 'He asked his men to drag me to his home and beat me. After this point I was beaten worse than animals. His men started kicking me, punching me, slapping me. They hit me wherever they could. Soon my entire body was enveloped in fresh blood dripping from my wounds. Then one of them, his name was Raavan, he tore my clothes and pushed the barrel of a gun in my urinary tract. I fainted and collapsed on the ground. I blacked-out for a couple of minutes.' Neelam adds that she felt a deep vibrating sound piercing her ears. Those vibrations and that deep piercing sound never left her. Till date, she often wakes from sleep feeling that same bass sound in her ears.

Struggling to keep her eyes open and trying hard to not lose track of the events happening to her, Neelam soon found herself at the local police station. 'I got to know that Dwivedi had levelled false charges of theft against me and I had been arrested for the same. Around 8 pm, I was taken to Naraini jail. The MLA threatened me again and said that if I didn't confess to the charges of theft, he will kill me. I had already had enough by now. I kept quite at that point of time. But later when I was produced in court, I cried my heart out and told everything to the judge. By now, the media also got to know and things started slipping away from his hands.'

The crime shook the country and hit the headlines.

With major Congress and Samajwadi Party leaders pitching in speeches and statements in favour of Neelam, the matter immediately took a political turn. The then chief minister of Uttar Pradesh, Mayawati, first expelled Purushottam Naresh Dwivedi from the party and a month later issued orders for Neelam's release from jail. She also ordered the state's crime branch to investigate the crime.

Later, the crime branch filed a chargesheet against Purushottam Naresh, Raavan, Virendra Garg, Suresh Mehta alias Raghuvanshi Dwivedi, Rajendra Shukla and five other accused.

Senior lawyer Harish Salve filed a public interest litigation (PIL) in the Supreme Court in 2012 demanding an independent judicial probe into the matter. In the hearing on his appeal, the apex court handed over the matter to the CBI. In addition to all sections mentioned in the previous chargesheet, the CBI booked Dwivedi for rape under Section 376 of the Indian Penal Code (IPC).

Both Dwivedi and Raavan's bail pleas were rejected multiple times by different courts during the course of the trial.

In June 2015, a CBI special court in Lucknow pronounced the judgment in this matter. In this landmark conviction, the court found Dwivedi guilty of rape. He was sentenced to 10 years of rigorous imprisonment. His aides Ram Naresh Dwivedi alias Raavan and Virendra Kumar Shukla alias Garg were each sentenced to two years of imprisonment.

Since then, several prominent leaders of the BJP, Congress and SP have paid visits to Neelam's mud hut. The list includes Rahul Gandhi, Jaya Prada, Smriti Irani, Rita Joshi Bahuguna and Vivek Singh. Many political parties also extended financial help. But, during the course of fighting this mammoth battle, she feels she has lost a great deal of herself.

Her family did stand by her in the beginning, but today they do not even want to talk to her. Quietly sobbing, she says, 'I am only waiting for justice, didi. Once I get it, I will go away from here. Nobody talks to me in this village... my father, my brother, my relatives, my neighbours... no one talks to me. They have all deserted me. That is why I live alone in this hut while my family lives together close by. My family feels bad that there are policemen standing outside my hut to give me protection. They feel embarrassed that politicians and media persons visit me. All of them think that I raised my voice a bit too loudly against the injustice done to me. But you tell me didi, is there a softer way to protest against something like this? I have been through hell. I have suffered so much to get justice. I was made to repeat my statements so many times in court and I repeated them. Even the villagers and other people from my community are not pleased that I am fighting this hard. But how can I not fight for justice after what was done me? Even now, my body aches. When I was in jail, the blood didn't stop flowing for 20 days. I went without food for 15 days. I didn't even get any medical treatment in the beginning. All the stitch marks are still there on my urinary tract. They tore apart my body. How can I forget this? Now, if I am left fighting this battle alone, let it be so. But I will fight it till the very end.'

During my interview with her, Neelam kept on slipping into different mental zones. Quite understandably so. Just after saying some of her most powerful sentences, she would retreat into her own cocoon. She was brave and I deeply felt her courage. But at the same time, I could see the physical pain and mental agony that she was suffering from.

Toward the end of the interview she talked about her future dreams. All she wanted was to live 'a normal life'. 'I don't have anything to do with these political parties. I am only waiting for my judgment. Once I get justice, I will go away from this village. I will go to some big metro city where nobody knows me. So many people earn their living in cities by working hard. I will also work hard; I will carry soil, I will put bricks in construction buildings, I will do anything but I will earn a living for myself. All I am looking for is a normal life, some love and peace.'

Around six months after the verdict came, Neelam contested in the gram panchayat elections from her village, fighting for the position of gram pradhan (village head). She lost and with 152 votes, stood at the fourth position in the results.

～

It was a hot afternoon in June 2013. At a busy public square in Uttar Pradesh's capital city Lucknow, I stood waiting for her. A couple of minutes later, we were exchanging phone calls and telling each other names of major ATMs and juice shops in the vicinity to help us locate each other. We had never met before so we did not recognize each other. She told me that she was wearing a parrot green printed cotton salwar kameez. In a few minutes I saw her walking towards me. I clearly remember that moment. Neatly side-parted hair weaved into a long braid and a smile on her face. She was holding books wrapped in an old polythene bag in her hands. Simple, confident and warm—this was the (then) 21-year-old Zahira standing in front of me. She lived at the other end of the city. We stopped an auto and hopped in immediately to start our almost hour long commute towards her home.

On 2 May 2005, Zahira was kidnapped and raped by six men in a moving car in Lucknow. She was only 13 then. A scrap-seller's daughter, Zahira used to work as a domestic help to make ends meet. On the fateful night of the crime, she was returning home after finishing her day's work in one of the houses situated in the Ashiana area of Lucknow. She was picked up by four men in a moving car. Two more joined later. The child was subjected to numerous cigarette burns and the barrel of a gun was forced into her private parts. Five hours and unimaginable amounts of cyclic violence later, she was dumped on the side of a deserted road in the Daliganj area of the city. Left alone to die.

The incident sent shockwaves across India and was seen as the first major urban case of sexual violence against women which involved a list of politically influential and financially powerful accused, including two juveniles. Later known as the 'Ashiana gang-rape', this case went on to become the first sustained urban battle against sexual violence in post-liberalization India.

But none of the above crossed my mind as I shared my auto ride with Zahira. For a while she talked about the important landmarks of Lucknow that we were passing. But she was silent for the rest of the time, her school books clutched in her hands. In June 2013, she was standing at the edge of what would go on to be an eight year old painfully long legal battle for justice, but it had not damaged her inherently kind spirit.

Zahira's family migrated to Lucknow from Assam decades ago in search of a better life. The family is still not fluent in Hindi, with the exception of Zahira, who learned to speak Hindi over the years. Language came up as a big problem for the family during the trial. With her deep Bengali/Assamese accent, explaining her ordeal to the police officers and legal authorities of Uttar Pradesh was a struggle. But with rounds and rounds of hearings going on for years, she has gotten better with the language over time.

Just a couple of minutes before we reached her residence, Zahira told me that during the course of the trial, a woman once approached her posing as a member of a women's commission. She asked her to put her thumb impressions on blank papers and promised that this will help her get compensation money. Later, Zahira realized that it was a trap set up by the accused. 'Those papers were used against me in court to delay the trial. I was unlettered till then. But that day I decided that I will study and learn how to read. I think I want to become a judge one day so that I can expedite the judicial process and deliver quick judgments to victims of rape.'

She wiped her tears silently and blankly gazed into nothingness. As I looked at her face lost in thoughts, a moment of silence slipped between. After a while we got out of the auto and started walking towards her residence.

On the way she talked a little about her desire to read. 'As soon as one of my tuition teachers got to know that I am the Ashiana gang-rape survivor, she refused to teach me. Why do people behave like this with me?' she asked me with the ingenuity of a child. I looked at the tears slowly settling down in the waterline of her eyes. At a loss for words, I felt an unaccountably heavy weight in my stomach and started looking down at the soil beneath our feet. After this we quietly walked to her house.

Zahira lives with her parents and siblings in a small two-room house in Lucknow. The atmosphere in the house is dark and morose. The walls are all rugged with seepage patches showing all around. A small old defunct cooler was standing idle as the family tried to keep themselves alive in the June heat of North India with the help of one ceiling fan. The family has survived abject poverty and the long legal battle has only made things worse. But the family is together in this battle and their resolve for justice is no less than steel. Zahira sits with her parents on the only bed in her house and we start the conversation.

On 2 May 2005, Zahira was returning home from work in the evening along with her five-year-old brother. As they reached the main road of the Ashiana colony, four men came in a Santro and dragged her inside.

Zahira recounts, 'Before I could make sense of anything, they had already rolled up the window and sped off. Initially there were four men. Then near Nishatganj, two more joined them. Then six of them together tore my clothes off. They were abusing me at the top of their voices. And, I remember—they were all laughing. Then they started watching obscene videos on their mobiles. They made me watch it too. Then hit me and burnt me with cigarettes. They threw me on the floor beneath the back seat. I was scared and crying hysterically all the time. I was begging them to let me go but no one was listening to me. They were all shouting loudly among themselves. After this they took turns to scratch and pinch me. The more I begged and cried, the harder they slapped, punched and kicked me. They pulled at my hair and started plucking my nails. They kept the beating on as they raped me one by one. They even had a gun. Gaurav Shukla and his friends hit me on my head with the gun's barrel. After this they inserted the gun inside my urinary tract and burned the area with cigarettes. I was bleeding profusely and was almost unconscious. It's all very hazy and blurred after this. I was in a lot of pain.'

Sitting next to her mother, Zahira is strikingly determined and composed now. She goes on to say, 'After this I remember that the car reached a farm house. They pulled me out of the car and dragged me into the farm house in that naked state. After this they threw me on the bed and all of them were on me. They were gnawing and chewing every part of my body. They were constantly beating me, abusing me, burning me with cigarettes. Then I heard Gaurav Shukla talk to someone on the phone. He was saying, "If you've brought the girl, then kill her after the work is done." I thought they were going to kill me. But they actually left me to die on the roadside.'

Later as the case hit headline, six men were arrested as accused of the the Ashiana gang-rape case. Their names were—Gaurav Shukla, Faizan, Asif Siddiqui, Bhartendu Misra, Saurabh Jain and Aman Bakshi. Initially all the accused claimed that they were minors when the crime happened. But the court rejected their applications in this regard. Out of the six accused, Asif Siddiqui and Saurabh Jain were declared to be juveniles. But they both died in separate road accidents in 2013. While Bhartendu Misra and Aman Bakshi were sentenced to 10 years imprisonment in 2007, Faizan was awarded life imprisonment in January 2013.

But the main accused in the case, Gaurav Shukla, evaded the trial for a long period by putting revision petitions in

different courts about his age to prove that he was a minor at
the time of the crime. Gaurav is a relative of the Samajwadi
Party (SP) leader Arun Shankar Shukla. A close associate of
SP supremo Mulayam Singh Yadav, Arun Shankar also has a
criminal background.

Madhu Garg, the Uttar Pradesh head of Rashtriya Janvadi
Mahila Sangathan, has been standing with Zahira and her
family in their fight for justice since Day One. During an
interview in her Lucknow office she says, 'It is clearly a poor
family's struggle against the political and criminal mafia of UP.
By using their money and power, they have been manipulating
and dragging the case for the past eight years now. Initially,
they made every effort to prove the main accused Gaurav is a
juvenile. His school records were changed, a fake certificate of
Chaya Public School was prepared and they even attempted
to seize his birth certificate from Lucknow Municipal
Corporation. Then his lawyers proved him a juvenile in a
forged case, and tried to use the same judgment in this case.
They have been pressurizing Zahira's family for a long time
now. Either by using money or power and threats. Every
time the lower court passes a judgment, they approach the
higher courts to challenge that order. This cycle has been
going on and on since past eight years. Looks like the whole
case has now become centred on proving that Gaurav was
not a juvenile while committing the crime. He has a battery
of lawyers who are known for dragging cases for decades. He
openly asks Zahira's father in the court, "How long will you
fight?" Their strategy is to tire down the victim's family. Zahira
has been summoned 26 times to face direct interrogation till
now. She has been consistent with her statements throughout.'

Madhu feels that the courage of Zahira and her father must
be saluted as they have been standing strong in the face of a

long torturous and tedious trial. 'If it is taking us so long to get justice even with all the pressure that media and civil society has been putting, one can imagine the hopeless situation of many other victims who cannot even come out in the open to speak about the violence done to them.'

Madhu has been working hard to ensure that Zahira continues with her education though it's difficult for her to join a regular school. Despite this brave fight that she has been putting up with all her courage, the social stigma associated with rape never leaves her. 'People call me names,' she tells me with lowered eyes. 'They say, "*Woh Ashiana rape wali ladki aa gayi*" (Look, that Ashiana rape victim has come).'

Before leaving, I ask Zahira's father's feelings about the punishment that the accused have been receiving so far. Zahira is sitting quietly next to him.

With his deep watery eyes, the father looks at me. He slowly gathers himself and replies in his broken Hindi, 'You see, a woman has two separate holes in the private parts of her body. One is for urine and menstruation to pass, and the other is for her body waste to pass through. When a barrel of a gun is inserted in your 13-year-old daughter in such a way that both these holes of her body become one, and then her wound is further burnt with cigarettes, what punishment would you demand for this crime? If your child returns home one night and her body is all burnt with cigarettes, slashed with blades and if her nails are all plucked, and she is all soaked in blood, what punishment would you ask for? Is there any way we can get justice for what we have gone through? No justice will ever reduce our pain. We die every day while Gaurav Shukla is free and now even married. No matter what they do, fill my house with treasures or shoot me, I won't back off. Even if I have to sell everything for it, I'll do it, but I'll fight till the end.'

## Postscript

On 19 April 2016, after an 11-year-long legal battle, Gaurav
Shukla was finally found guilty. He was convicted by a
Lucknow sessions court and sentenced for 10 years of rigorous
imprisonment. His lawyers have appealed in higher courts
against the lower court judgment. While Zahira's family is
happy that they have finally got closure, they do feel that
justice reached them too late and delivered too little.

# 5

# In the Dark

## In custody rapes

AS A REPORTER, I FEEL, FEW NARRATIVES HAVE THE POWER
to drag you out of the utopian urban islands full of chiseled
conversations about 'progress' and 'equality' and 'the struggle
for it' and warm beds and warmer glasses of alcohol. These
narratives then directly transport you out of your imagined
reality and drop you into a messy, muddy universe which you
cannot even imagine existed; till you see it with your own eyes.

After being dropped in this parallel universe which
actually exists within the geographical boundaries of your
own country—your own free, independent country run by a
Constitution which was written on the principles of equality
and justice and inclusive growth for all—you feel dazed for
the initial few minutes. But you somehow try to stand up on
your feet and start walking.

While walking you quickly realize a fact that this 'parallel
universe' actually exists right in the centre of your 'free
independent country'. It exists 'right below' and it exists 'all
around' the urban islands of Delhi, Bombay, etc.—places
where the urban elite live in clean houses, built in posh

colonies having clean wide roads, go to shit in fragrant clean toilets and then come out to read a newspaper story on 'How quickly India is becoming open defecation free country!'

Now if you are an urban kid and if you are dropped into this 'parallel universe' for the first time, you might feel a little shocked at every step. As rootless as I am, I never belonged anywhere ever in the true sense. So I always felt more disgusted and less shocked.

For example, how will you feel if in the middle of 2015 you happen to walk into a village in Uttar Pradesh and get to know that two policemen just picked up a 14-year-old minor girl—right from in front of her own house—shoved her in their 'police jeep', took her to the nearest police chowki and raped her for four hours and then dropped her a few hundred yards away from her house with a threat that she and her whole family will be killed if she dares to opens her mouth?

It's not over yet. Villagers tell you that the girl had stepped out of her house to pee. He mother was also with her. They had to step out to pee because there are NO toilets in the whole village which has a population of roughly 1500 Indian citizens now.

Not over yet.

There are NO approach roads and NO electricity in this village.

No electricity? You might repeat this question in your head in disbelief. Are the wires and connections not working?

'No, madame, we don't have any electric poles here. Electricity never reached our village. A couple of villagers use solar electricity panels. But they also cost a lot and everybody cannot afford them. So we live in the dark here.'

No roads, no electricity, no toilets. Policemen abducting girls from their own homes, gang-raping them and threatening to end their lives if they opened their mouths. You look at your phone to check if you are really only seven hours and 260 kilometres away from Delhi in the year 2015 or have you landed in Afghanistan by mistake?

Not over yet.

You are told that the minor girl's father died just 10 days after the crime took place—due to 'shame'. HE—I mean the father of the victim—felt ashamed, and HE died of that 'shame'.

One villager standing under a huge tree said, 'He was a pandit and would go to all nearby villages to perform different poojas at people's houses. People used to call him for doing pooja whenever a child was born or someone was getting married or if someone died. He was our local priest. That is why he felt very ashamed.'

You notice how the man stresses on the word 'shame'. This villager I have been talking to is a neighbour and also a distant relative of the victim's family. At least 10 more men have gathered around him; they all live in the neighbourhood and have known the victim's family for years. They all nod their heads in agreement with this villager who can't be named here.

This villager is in his early 40s, wearing a worn out off-white shirt with brown stripes and loose dark brown trousers. He has a torn pair of black rubber slippers on and his feet were covered in multiple layers of mud and dirt.

'The girl's father stopped eating after the incident. Would only keep repeating, "*Mera mooh kala ho gaya, ab main kisi ko kya mooh dikhaunga?*" (My face has been blackened. How will I go out and face people with this black face now?). He refused to eat, sulked and cried for 10 days and then suddenly died on the 11th day,' he continued. 'The family is in a deep crisis. The girl feels that she should have died instead of her father. But god's will is the highest will. And anyway what is anyone's death going to change in any case now? *Jo hona tha woh ho chuka* (What had to happen has happened). *Izzat...* pride... is all we poor people have. If our pride is gone, everything is gone.'

My mind is a mess. I feel numb.

I am still sitting in the outer verandah of the girl's house. Still haven't stepped inside, still haven't met her or any of her family members. I am told to wait for five more minutes outside. But before even entering her house, I have all the above details in my mind and I already have a memory of the incident now.

How is 'honour' bigger than the life of any individual? Who made these rules? Men made these rules? The rules about thrusting a family's honour in the vagina of the women of the family? I want to say—a woman is more than her vagina. But I don't.

~

It's the last week of April in the year 2015. The sun has started burning the northern Indian plains like a charcoal furnace.

As I wait outside, I think of the conversations I just had with the villagers. I also think of my journey today. I left my rented accommodation in Delhi at around 4 am in the morning and travelled for seven hours in a hired car to reach this point—this village in the Dataganj Tehsil of the Badaun district of Uttar Pradesh. I feel I have crossed two worlds in just 260 kilometres.

This village also comes under the Aonla Lok Sabha constituency. Bhartiya Janta Party's Maneka Gandhi won this seat in 2009 and Dharmendra Kashyap from her party became her successor to the seat in 2014. I am mentioning this here because Maneka Gandhi did gave a statement to the press condemning the in-custody gang-rape of the minor girl and asked for stern action to be taken against the cops.

The story did not make national headlines and I suppose very few people outside Uttar Pradesh even got to know about the incident. But in the state, the local press did run a couple of follow-ups and the then chief minister of the state—Akhilesh Yadav—assured action against the accused.

In an ideal world the administration's action should have started with the arrests of the accused and by slapping charges under The Protection of Children from Sexual Offenses (POCSO) Act plus additional charges of abduction and rape on them.

In reality, it actually started with the mere 'dismissal' of the two accused cops, Avnish Yadav and Veerpal Yadav, from their duties and the suspension of Musaganj police station in-charge at the time of crime—SHO Ram Lakhan Singh Yadav. The arrests of the accused did happen, but that came much later.

But 'what should happen in an ideal world' is as dreamy a fantasy as the ideal world itself is.

I think of the father who saw a crime that 'happened' to her daughter as 'his own' fault—his own shame. My mind goes back to some of my past conversations with other colleagues and editors back in Delhi. We were debating the use of the word 'victim' in news reports. 'We should stop using the word 'victim' and use 'survivor' instead,' I remember one of my editors suggested during a conversation.

Though important, such a conversation appears so far away and distant from the ground beneath my feet right now. This remote village in Badaun makes the wide-wide valley of inequality in India come alive in front of my eyes in all its ugliness. The wide gap between the haves and have-nots; the gap which is making the rich richer and the poor poorer.

There is no place for 'book-marked niceties' like 'justice' and 'the victim versus survivor debate' or 'stop blaming the victim' discourse here in this part of India. I feel a scathing lawlessness spreading everywhere. And if you lose your sense of geography and memory for a minute, you might believe that you are standing in a Taliban-controlled remote village of Afghanistan or in a war-torn tribal African village existing some 50 years back in time.

It's only when you regain your lost consciousness that you realize that this is happening today, roughly 70 years after Independence in an Indian state under a democratically elected government.

~

I meet the victim's 42-year-old mother as soon as I enter the house. We greet each other with folded hands. She is wearing an orange sari with the pallu of the sari completely covering her head and hair. Fodder for a cow that the family rears is kept in huge mountainous stacks just adjacent to the main entrance door. There are a couple of cheap plastic chairs lying around. Most of the men from the neighbourhood whom I was talking to outside have stepped inside the house and settled themselves down on the plastic chairs. I was standing at the centre of the inner courtyard of the house. The victim's mother stood silently next to me and asked if I would like some water.

And the very next moment she suddenly started sobbing and told me that she can't talk in front of so many people. I requested the men sitting in the courtyard to step out of the house for a couple of minutes. They nodded, albeit a bit reluctantly, and started walking out.

The mother held my hand and walked me in. Across the

courtyard, we walked to reach the two-room set where the family lived. I was asked to sit on a wooden stool. The mother sat on a string cot lying in front of me. The 14-year-old girl, her eldest child was also sitting on that cot. An 11-year-old boy, her younger son and the girl's brother, was sitting on the floor nearby. An old printed georgette sari had been turned into a makeshift curtain for the room. Now there were only the four of us in that space. The survivor, her mother, her younger brother and me.

The first thing I noticed in the girl was her eyes. I clearly remember to this day—her deep big eyes that spoke. She was lying on the cot with her head turned to the other side of the wooden head-rail and her gaze fixed towards the ceiling of the house. Her long hair hanging from the side of the cot was touching the ground. Her body language was that of a regular 14-year-old kid but her eyes had the sadness and vulnerability of an adult who had seen too much suffering at a very young age.

The child kept weeping throughout. She was in her personal space, trying to deal with her grief on her own. So I did not ask her any question. She did not speak a single word to me. We just looked at each other in silence.

But her mother spoke.

'It was the first night of 2015—1 January 2015. Pitch dark all around except for the oil lamps that we use here. Around 9 pm in the night, my daughter told me that she wants to pee. I burned a fresh lamp and took her out of the house. Normally we walk a little far from our houses and pee in the nearby fields. But since it was very cold and dark outside, I asked her to pee just across the road in front of our house. She went to pee and I was standing guard just a few feet away. Just then we saw the police jeep approaching. It slowed down near us,

I heard a cry of "Mummy" but before I could reach they had dragged her in and driven away. I still hear her voice crying for help in my dreams. She would be screaming "Mummy Mummy" in the dream but every time I fail to reach her before waking up from the dream.'

The mother was sobbing again by now. But she continued to speak while her tears and hiccups kept interspersing with her words.

'I started shouting and howling and ran to fetch my neighbours. But no one could gather the courage to go to the police station. The cops took my daughter away, how could we approach THEM? I froze and my mind stopped working. At that point, there was no one at home except me and this little 11-year-old boy of mine. My husband was in Bareilly for an eye operation. Then someone from the neighbourhood called him and I told him what happened on the phone. His first response was, "*Wo le kaise gaye ladki ko? Ham maar dalenge tumko wapas aakar!*" (How did they take away the girl? I will kill you when I return for letting this happen!).'

The parents were both baffled and scared. The father had undergone an eye operation the day before. He said he wouldn't be able to reach the village before morning. This was the longest night for this family. No one in the neighbourhood had the courage to go to the nearest police station to look for the girl or for reporting the matter. Everyone just kept waiting.

I was told that the two accused cops were notorious and teased men and women passing through the village for work every day. 'When we would ask why they are spending hours sitting idly under trees in the village, they would say that they are protecting the village and looking out for goons. We trusted them because they were from the police. But now we can join the dots,' a village elder had told me in a conversation outside the house.

Four hours later, the girl came home.

'I was sitting at the door waiting when post-midnight I saw her walking towards the house. She was crying and limping. I brought her inside the house and closed all doors. She had scratch marks all over her body and she was bleeding. We both kept crying. My daughter said, "It's better that you kill me now, Mummy. Instead of going to the police, kill me".'

The daughter lying next to her on the same cot was listening. Suddenly she started to sob and mumbled, '*Hamaare papa ki jagah ham hi mar jaate to accha hota, ham kyon nahi mar gaye?* (It would have been better if I had died instead of my father. Why did I not die in his place?)'

I felt numb.

The mother went on, 'Her father came home next morning and we went to the police station in Badaun city. We were humiliated and forced to compromise at first. But later when the media came in, then finally our complaint was registered. But her father could not bear all this... this burden of shame. He was a well-known priest in his neighbourhood. He would repeat only one line to me—"How will I step out with this black face?" I think he could imagine his face as really black. He felt ashamed that his honour was gone. Who will marry our daughter now? We have no face left in the society.' She starts wailing looking at both her children who are crying.

As I walk out of the house, I think to myself how can being the victim of a crime lead to shame? Why are the accused not ashamed? Why are these people not shaming the accused? Shame is in raping a woman, not in being raped.

But in many parts of our country fathers are still dying and daughters are wishing for their own deaths—especially in rural India—because of the shame associated with rape.

## Version 2.0: Black Holes

NASA's official website describes a 'black hole' as 'a place in space where gravity pull is so much that even light cannot get out. The gravity is so strong because matter has been squeezed into a tiny space. This can happen when a star is dying. Because no light can get out, people can't see black holes.'

I feel that the situation of women in India is like these black holes in space: dying stars. No one can see these black holes because obviously no light is allowed to pass through us.

If the above analogy sounds exaggerated to you, sample this: You are a mother whose 14-year-old daughter has been sexually assaulted and then brutally killed inside the premises of the police station near your home. You run around your village looking for your missing child and when you finally find her, her body is hanging from a tree standing in the police station compound.

You feel like you are trapped in a blind well. You lose your sense of time and geography. You feel that you are going round and round and round and round and round in that blind well. You feel as if you are going to die. But then you hold the body of your dead child in your hands and try to escape the trappings of the blind well. You make rounds of the courts, lawyers, higher police stations and plead for justice. You howl. You want to fight the case and get justice for your daughter. But then, hey! There is another blind well waiting for you.

The people around you feel that you are raising your voice a bit too loudly. You are asking 'too much' for justice. Now, the mother of the victim, it's time for your character assassination to start. You own husband who is also the father of your child who was raped and murdered is the first one to object. He says that you are 'going out too much' and making 'too many rounds' of the police station, meeting 'too many men who are lawyers' and that all this is not good. He accuses you of being 'well dressed', 'stepping out of the house' and 'talking to other men in the garb of seeking justice for your daughter'. The fact that you are married to him for years and bore him seven children makes no difference. When the husband starts speaking ill of you, everyone else joins in. Your neighbours accuse you of being a woman with a bad character. They tell their wives and daughters to not speak to you or to come under your influence. False and fabricated stories about how you are having affairs with police officers and how you carry lunch for them start floating in the village. Your husband does not want you to step out of the house and if you must go out in an emergency he disapproves of your saying 'namaste' to anyone you come across on the way.

A can of worms has opened up against you. You feel that all this hostility is choking you and you think to yourself—where were these worms hiding when your daughter was being raped and murdered?

You again feel that you are going round and round and round and round and round in another blind well. There is just no escape.

No light is passing through us. So nobody can see all this happening to us.

That is why, we are all black holes. Facing one blind well waiting for another.

Dying stars.

~

I travel around 450 kilometres away from Delhi to reach the Nighasan police station area in the Lakhimpur Kheri district of Uttar Pradesh. Almost a 10 hours' drive by road from

Delhi, Lakhimpur Kheri is the largest district of Uttar Pradesh. Situated on the northern tip of the state, it shares one side of its border with Nepal. The highways were patchy in parts but smooth for the larger part of my road trip to Nighasan.

I stopped around 200 metres before the Nighasan police station and waited in the car. It was mid-April, 2015. The weather was humid and hot. But as you move towards Nepal, the burning sensation of the afternoon sun is a little less scathing.

After a couple of minutes, I could see 40-year-old Rabiya walking towards me. She was wearing an orange sari, her head and hair all covered with her pallu. We exchanged greetings and decided to have a detailed conversation at her house. But before that, she wanted to show me something.

We both started walking towards the Nighasan police station. A large part of the building was newly constructed and painted. As we entered, I saw a couple of policemen hanging around in the courtyard of the building. Rabiya did not looked up or greet any one of them. She kept looking down at her feet and walking ahead. I followed her. She took me to the backyard of the police station and raised her finger towards an old dilapidated building lying abandoned a few metres ahead of us in the backyard. There was an abandoned tractor lying next to this decaying, eerie building. And there were plants and greenery growing unchecked around the abandoned tractor as well as the ramshackle concrete structure.

She pointed her finger towards the ruins and said, 'This is the building where Nighasan police station used to exist in June 2011. My daughter was found hanging from a tree in this compound. They raped her, murdered her and then hanged her from a tree in the compound to make it look like a suicide. After the matter came out and charges were framed, the government constructed a new building which you now see working as the Nighasan police station.'

~

As we started walking away from the police station towards Rabiya's house, I kept looking at her. She came across as a confident and warm woman in the first few minutes. It was only later during our conversation at her house that I discovered the many layers of courage, vulnerability and steel-like strength inside her.

It took a brisk walk of five minutes to reach Rabiya's house from the Nighasan police station—a two-room red-brick construction standing on its own without any cement, plaster or paint. She walked me in to the front room of the house. There was an old bed and two plastic chairs lying around. Her husband, 45-year-old Imtiyaz, was sitting on the bed.

As Rabiya offers a glass of water to me, I could see tears brimming at the edge of her kohl-laced eyes.

'I had seven children. Now after Zoya, six are left. Three boys and three girls. Zoya was my second born. And she was a lovely child, very close to my heart. Maybe I loved her more because she was destined to leave us early. But I never imagined that she will leave us like she did.'

Rabiya is crying now. I am sitting silently next to her. I want to hold her hand but I feel like I will intrude in her grief. I request the husband to fetch a glass of water for her. He leaves the room and I sit quietly, waiting for her to feel a little better. Rabiya's gaze is fixed on the wall before her. There is nothing on the wall. She is lost in her thoughts.

After a couple of minutes she speaks again.

'10 June 2011 was the date. Hindus were holding a huge pooja in the village and for us it was an important prayer day of the week—a Friday. So everyone everywhere was in a bit of a rush that morning in the village. We had a buffalo in our house and she had given birth recently. Around 10 am that morning, the calf somehow got running. My 14-year-old daughter Zoya ran after the animal. Her three-year-old brother also ran after her. The calf entered the police station compound and my children entered the compound, running behind it. After that point, both my children went missing. When they did not come back for one hour, we started looking for them. They were nowhere in the village. We looked everywhere. After three or four hours, my youngest son who went missing with Zoya came home running. He was crying and sweating. He told me that Zoya is at the police station. I ran towards the police station. There was a house constructed next to the boundary wall of the police station compound. I entered this house and peeped inside the police station compound from the boundary wall. I could see her sitting down under the tree. A white duppata was tied around her neck and then to the branch of the tree. From a distance, she looked like she was sitting in Namaz. I had no idea that she was dead. I thought she was sitting. I immediately jumped from the boundary wall and ran towards my daughter. I touched her back and said, "Zoya... Zoya!'"

~

But Zoya did not answer.

Her tongue was protruding out of her mouth and her eyes were open. She was wearing loose black pants and a ragged old off-white t-shirt. The moment her mother touched her back, her body collapsed in her arms.

'I was devastated. I started screaming and shouting. The villagers heard and people started gathering inside the police station compound. Everyone was watching the show but no one helped me. The policemen came out of the police station and asked me to take away the dead body of my daughter. I refused to lift her body from the ground and accused them of killing my daughter. But they threatened to kill me and said, *"Jaise teri ladki ki laash giraayi hai waise hi teri bhi gira denge"* (We will kill you just like we have killed your daughter).'

Zoya's father was not at home at the time of this incident. A wedding was scheduled in his extended family and he was distributing invitation cards in neighbouring villages. Meanwhile, Rabiya lifted her daughter's dead body in her arms and walked home alone.

'The moment she collapsed in my hands didi, the moment I realized that she was dead—something changed inside me. I still don't know how I lifted her up in my arms and brought her home. The whole village had gathered in front of my house but no one would touch the body of my daughter because it was a matter in which the police station was involved. Everybody was scared of the cops. But she was my daughter. I pulled the curtain on the main door and removed every piece of cloth on her body. I saw her with my own eyes. She was bleeding down there. Her right leg was slightly deformed and uplifted. Her teeth looked like they were chattering. There were scratch marks, nail marks and bite marks all over her breasts and thighs. I knew instantly she was raped. My youngest son later told me that they took him and Zoya inside the side room in the police chowki. There they laid her on the cot and assaulted her. The boy was made to stand right there and was beaten up to keep quiet.'

~

The memory and narration of a three-year-old child can be faulty but scientific reports and evidence don't lie. As the

matter came to light, it immediately shot into the national
headlines. All 11 policemen present at the Nighasan police
station on the day of the crime were suspended.

Post-mortem report said that the girl committed suicide.
The family alleged that it was a cover-up to protect the cops.
After the media glare, another post-mortem was conducted
and it concluded murder by strangulation as the cause of
Zoya's death. All the doctors who conducted the first post-
mortem of the girl were eventually suspended.

Rabiya tells me stories about how she was pressurized by
the local administration and police to back out. 'They first said
that my daughter committed suicide. But gave no reason why.
Why will my playful cheerful child kill herself? She woke up
smiling that morning. Perhaps she did not even know what
killing means. When the Crime Investigation Department-
CID (CB-CID) started investigating the case, they refused
to give me any detail or any paper related to the case. When
I went to ask for copies of the FIR and post-mortem report,
they treated me like a dog. They would shoo me away. Earlier,
local police officers had offered me five lakh rupees to settle
the case. I said I will give you 10 lakh, can you bring back my
daughter? Are our children out there for sale?'

With the visits of Rahul Gandhi and Akhilesh Yadav to
Rabiya's house, demands of a CBI enquiry started gaining
voice. 'Rahul Bhaiya and Akhilesh Bhaiya came to my house
and assured me that my daughter will get justice. Since the
local police is involved and tried to bribe me, I had no hopes
of a fair investigation from them. I was demanding a fair
enquiry from a higher investigative agency for a long time.
But my request was considered only after Rahul Bhaiya and
Akhilesh Bhaiya visited our house. After that all big officers
started coming in from the district headquarters and soon our
case was handed over to the CBI.'

## The prime accused

Three weeks after Zoya was killed, the then cabinet secretary of Uttar Pradesh, Shashank Shekhar Singh, told reporters in a press conference that a constable named Atique Ahmed has confessed to the crime. Atique was attached to the circle officer of Kheri as his gunner at that time.

Press was informed that the constable killed the girl after she raised an alarm. 'On June 10, the constable tried to lure the girl and started sexually assaulting her. But when she raised an alarm and started shouting, he strangulated her with her dupatta... Thereafter, the gunner offered "namaz" and then hanged the girl's body from a tree in the police station,' he said.

Initial investigations by the state police's special investigative agency CB-CID suggested that the girl was murdered by constable Atique inside his room in the police station.

Later, the CBI took over the case from the CB-CID and filed charges against five police officers—sexual assault, murder and then trying to cover up the case by portraying it as a suicide. The five cops charge-sheeted in this case are: Atique Ahmed, Shiv Kumar, Uma Shankar, Ram Chandra and Ayotullah Khan. They were all on duty at the Nighasan police station on the morning of the incident. Atique Ahmed remains the prime accused in the case.

~

As the trial goes on in the CBI court of Lucknow, blind wells of fresh battles have opened up for Rabiya.

Her husband complains to me that she is not paying attention to him, to the house and to the rest of her children due to Zoya's case. *'Ladki ka case ladne ka matlab ye to nahi ki bahar gair logon se milte raho aur ghar aur bacchon ko chod do!* (Does fighting the case of Zoya mean meeting unknown men every day and not paying attention to your own house and children!)'

I keep quiet.

Rabiya starts speaking again. She is crying once more and I can now see the second blind well in which she is circling clearly.

There is a rage in her voice when she says, '*Jab aurat aawaz uthaati hai, toh aadmi usko dabaata hai. Kyonki uska maqsad aurat ke nyaay ke liye ladna nahi hai. Wo sirf use ghar pe baandh ke rakhna chahta hai. Inko meri har baat se dikkat hai. Apni beti ke liye main nahi ladoongi to kaun ladega?* (When a woman raises her voice, a man tries to suppress her. Because the man is not concerned if the woman gets justice or not. All he is concerned with is keeping the women chained at home and under his control. If I will not fight for my daughter, then who will?)'

But clearly, Rabiya is also fighting for her own self as well. The rape and murder of her daughter has made her see the patriarchal chains tied to her feet.

While speaking of her daughter, Rabiya is full of anger and tears and fire. Yet she looks vulnerable, sad and beautiful.

~

The husband keeps mumbling and then walks away. Rabiya comes out of the house and walks with me till the main approach road of the village where my transport back to Delhi is waiting.

On the way she tells me that all kinds of attempts have been made to drag her away from the case.

'They said things like I was having affairs with the cops

and that I carry tiffin for them. My lawyer—he was also a Muslim like us—he called me one day and asked me to settle the case in exchange for a few lakhs. Atique Ahmed's parents came to my house four times. They tried to bribe me into settling too. But how could a mother make money out of her child's death? She was raped and killed by policemen, whom we trust with our lives, don't we?' She roars.

At this point she lowers her voice and whispers, 'My husband tells me that some older men in the family are advising him to remove the names of Muslim men from the complaint and keep only the Hindus in. How can I do that? Only a monster rapes and strangulates a child that small! No god-fearing Hindu or Muslim will do such a thing! So when I denied taking back the case at any cost, these people started calling me a bad woman. You tell me didi, if a woman speaks for her dead daughter, does that make her bad? Who will stand for my Zoya if not me?' she says looking at me with a thousand questions written on her face.

As we reach the car waiting for me, we stop and stand facing each other. I am at a loss for words. Too shocked, disgusted and hurt from inside to say anything. I just look at Rabiya and then I hug her.

She smiles.

Her smile gives me the courage to give her my number and ask her to call me if 'anyone troubles her too much'. She smiles again.

'I will try to do whatever little I can,' I say.

She smiles a little again and I keep looking at her—and the honesty of her spirit.

Before leaving, I don't know what comes over me, I get out of the car and walk up to her to say a final goodbye.

Requesting her to focus on the case and to not pay

any heed to the patriarchal bullshit being thrown at her by
the villagers, local cops, government officials and her own
husband, I say, 'They are not used to seeing a strong woman
like you walking around here. But you stay strong, Rabiya.
Chin and head up, always, Rabiya. I will pray for you and
your daughter.'

I fight back tears and rush to the car and drive away.

~

I remember getting missed calls from Rabiya a couple of times
after I reached Delhi. She would be very happy when I would
call back. She spoke of the case and told me that she wants
to move to the city after her daughter's judgment comes. She
was finding village life claustrophobic. I said she must and I
will come to pick her up from the station just like she came
to pick me up in Nighasan.

But over the years, I travelled frequently and lived outside
India for a couple of months. We changed numbers and lost
touch. I am keeping a track of Rabiya's daughter's case which
is still undergoing trial. I think I will go to see her again. May
be when the judgment comes out or maybe, earlier.

# 6

# The Anatomy of a Rape in Haryana

## The Bhagana gang-rape case

YOU CAN, IF YOU WISH TO, TRACE AN ALMOST DIRECT LINE from the dispute over a playground in the Bhagana village of Hisar district, Haryana, to the circumstances that have led to hundreds of Dalit families living in the open, outside a government building, for years. And an almost direct line from the playground to the circumstances that led to four young girls and their parents living for the last four months on the streets in central Delhi.

On the night of 23 March 2014, Janvi, Sushma, Leela and Meena were abducted from Bhagana and raped. Since 16 April 2014 they and their families have been at Jantar Mantar in New Delhi. While the whole country continues to obsess about sexual assault, the public eye has passed uncaring over the four girls sitting right in the centre of the capital. The seasons have changed—they came in blazing summer but they have stayed, hoping that in Delhi they will find what their village never gave them their whole lives.

~

In 2011, the gram sabha of the Bhagana village panchayat headed by Kitab Singh, a Dalit sarpanch, decided to distribute 280 acres of village land, including common land, amongst its residents. As *Frontline* reported, this move came in response to the Haryana government's announcement that it would distribute 100 square yards of land to every family living below the poverty line (BPL). The plan was scuttled by the new Jat sarpanch who came in, and land was instead distributed in proportion to the land that the village residents already owned. This meant that the landless Dalit families ended up with no land, or with less than 100 square yards each. The Dalits protested. The Jats retaliated. As *The Hindu* reported, 'Ponds which the Dalits used for drinking water and other purposes were dried up. A playground used predominantly by Dalit children was dug up. Access to roads for several Chamar households was blocked by erecting six-foot-high walls.' Things didn't stop there.

In February 2012, the Jats claimed the playground altogether (even though as Virendra Singh Bagoriya, a Dalit activist from the village and the leader of the Bhagana Kand Sangharsh Samiti says, the Jats had their own ground, which was much bigger). Next, a brick wall was built around the disputed land blocking the Dalit families' access to their own homes. They could not take their buffalos to the common village pond anymore. The shopkeepers stopped giving them rations. The barbers stopped cutting their hair and the village flour mills stopped grinding their wheat. The drinking water pipeline of the Dalit tola was blocked. Moreover, this boycott meant that the Dalits lost their livelihood, as the Jats would no longer employ them for any work.

In the summer of 2012, 138 Dalit families (mostly from the Chamar and Khanti communities) left for Hisar in protest. Since that day, for over two years, they have been sitting—men, women and children—in front of the Hisar mini-secretariat on an indefinite dharna. Around 150 Dalit families (all from the Dhanuk community) stayed put in Bhagana. And it's from among those families that four girls were abducted that summer.

During my reporting of the case in July 2014, in Bhagana village, when I was talking to Reetika, Janvi's older sister, a few other women from the neighbourhood gathered around us. Sixty-year-old Angoori Devi broke in and said, 'The Jats did this to our girls because they are angry that Dalits in this village were fighting for their rights on the village common land and playground. They hate us because we were raising our voices against them.'

I asked if Dalit girls from the village had ever played on the playground. Fifty-year-old Teeja Devi laughed and the others' grim faces broke into grins. A few minutes later Teeja recovered and said, 'I am laughing because your question is like asking a child who has never seen a ball in his whole life to kick a ball properly! Dalit girls don't step out of their doors. They've never stepped on this playground, forget about playing there! *Arrey*, when our girls stay inside their homes, even then these Jats kidnap them and rape them. Even small girls are teased and assaulted when they go to school. You can't imagine what will happen if our girls stepped on the playground! They will be abused and tortured to give a strong message so that no other girl can dare to step out in future. So no Dalit girl of this village has ever been on a playground. We are too scared to even think about this.'

She adds, 'Yes, old women like me, we used to go to the common village land to make dry gobar. But all our movements stopped after the Dalits were boycotted in 2012.

These girls have paid the price of Dalit resistance while many others among us have been routinely paying the price of being born as a Dalit woman in this village for ages now. If we get our playground back, only Dalit boys will be able to play, exercise and keep fit for getting work in the army or police or anywhere. Anyways, these girls will never play on it. Because Dalit girls play inside homes, not on playgrounds.' After a moment of frozen silence, she added, '*Ham to sirf maidan aur khel ki keemat chukayein hain, khelein kabhi na payein* (We only seem to pay the price for wanting the ground and to play, but cannot play ever).'

~

That afternoon in July 2014, when I arrived, 20-year-old Reetika is sitting on the mud verandah of her two-room house. Reetika and Janvi grew up with their two brothers in this small house situated in the Dhanuk (a Dalit sub-caste) basti. I'd walked through the Dalit tola of Bhagana to reach Reetika's house. Most of the houses stand locked and empty. Only 40 Dhanuk families still live in Bhagana.

That afternoon, Reetika is wearing a mustard yellow salwar kameez and a magenta dupatta. Her round face is stoic and she smiles. The small neem saplings her mother had planted have withered. Inside, the second room is still locked and the room she's been living in these last two days, since she came from her in-laws home, is dusty. The open *chulha* on which the family used to cook, on which Reetika used to cook before she got married, is now covered in thick dust, leftover ash, a few utensils and a broken bicycle.

'Our home and neighbourhood is now destroyed,' she tells me. 'Nothing is left. First, the Jats captured the common land of our village and boycotted all those Dalits who dared to resist. Then all the Chamars and Khantis left the village, while the Dhanuks stayed back. We could not gather the courage to leave our houses back then. Now, after this attack (on Janvi and the others girls), staying back was not an option. We knew that our lives were in danger in this village. My parents thought that we'd get justice, or at least be able to raise our voices against this crime only if we protested at Hisar or Jantar Mantar. So in mid-April they left the village along with 90 other Dhanuk families from our neighbourhood. Our tola has been deserted since then.'

Reetika's younger sister, 13-year-old Janvi, is the youngest of all the four survivors of the Bhagana gang-rape. She was kidnapped barely 500 metres away from her home along with Sushma (17), Leela (17) and Meena (18).

Reetika points her finger towards the now-deserted verandah and says, 'We grew up here. Since she was the youngest child of the family, she was always a bit pampered, but never more than my brothers. We would play together here, talk, laugh, cook and sometimes even fight. She had a few dolls and sometimes we ran around playing *juggo* in this verandah. When we grew up, we would cook, talk and occasionally watch TV serials together.'

Later she says, 'When I think about her now, all I feel is that she was too small, too fragile to go through such a brutal attack. My mother told me that she was in a bad condition when she returned home, after that night. She was partially conscious, her body was still bleeding and she was in severe pain. I know men routinely attack and abuse girls here, but still, I feel that she is too small to go through all this.'

Her despair is so deep—it's as if Reetika doesn't believe that Janvi's fate was wholly avoidable, only that it could have been delayed till she was older. The only reason that Reetika is

back here in this village is to represent her family at a wedding
in the extended clan. Life, she knows, goes on elsewhere. Even
if her own family is frozen in time in front of an 18th century
astronomy loving prince's toy.

Earlier that month in 2014, at Jantar Mantar, I'd spoken
to the young mothers of the survivors. There's no accounting
for the greater and lesser violence that these women have faced
over their lifetimes.

Of Bhagana village's 3,800 voters, 2,000 are Jats. Most
Dalits in this village are landless and earn their bread by
working on Jat-owned farms. They either work under the
*bataidari* system, under which they grow crops on Jat lands
and are allowed to keep only a small fixed percentage of the
produce, or they follow the *siri* system, under which a Dalit
does work on a Jat farm for a fixed period of time, and also
does domestic tasks for the Jat household during that period.

'In a way, the Dalit becomes a bonded labourer under the
Jat during this period. He has to do whatever work the Jat
says. And Jats make them do all kinds of menial jobs besides
making them work on the fields. Of course, the Jat owner
thinks that he has every right over the wives and daughters
of his Dalit bonded labourers. There have been many cases
in which Jats enter the homes of Dalits on any given night
and ask the man to step out, giving him some task such as
watering the fields. Then they sleep with their women. The
Dalit man who goes to water the fields knows what is going
on with his wife, but he can't do anything about this,' says
Bagoriya during an interview with me.

One evening, Sushma's mother Reshma tells me what
happened to her; the reason she thinks the girls were raped.
Her husband Vishnu used to be a bonded labourer for the
village sarpanch Rakesh Panghal. In January this year, she said,

her husband was working on the sarpanch's fields. It was a cold night and Vishnu fell asleep while watering the fields. A lot of water from the sarpanch's pump was wasted, and Reshma says the sarpanch beat up her husband twice and molested her as well. 'When my husband went to the government hospital in Hisar with blood flowing from his head, the doctors bandaged his wounds but refused to give him a written prescription or anything that we could have used for a police report.' He went to the Hisar superintendent of Police (SP) to file a complaint, but the SP advised her husband to arrive at a compromise with the sarpanch. Reshma says the enraged sarpanch threatened her husband and told him to be prepared to pay. Reshma thinks the rape of her daughter and the other four girls was their payment.

It's been raining at the protest camp at Jantar Mantar, but the rainfall has now stopped and the sky is a clear orange. The humidity soars again and the camp is muddy. At 4.30 pm, Janvi wants chai but her mother Bhagmati says that she will have to wait for an hour. Bhagmati and I talk about the day Janvi was born. While shifting bags of rations from the wet corners of the tent under which they're camped to the shrinking dry patch in the centre, she says, '*Hamaare gaon mein mahaul itna ganda hai ki ladki ke paida hone par sirf darr lagta hai. Ek to Dhanuk, upar se ladki; jaan kaise bacha paungi iski, yahi darr satata rehta tha.* (The environment of our village is so disgusting that we only feel scared whenever a girl is born in our community. First a Dhanuk, above that a girl! All my life I have been troubled by one question, how am I going to save the lives of my daughters?).'

Bhagmati and I are painfully conscious that Janvi is listening as her mother says of her youngest child, 'Everyone in my family (including me) was very sad when Janvi was born. We were terrorized by the thought that we had to look after one more daughter. I gave birth to three boys and two girls.' Bhagmati's panic about her daughters is not related to the reasons that led Haryana to have a low sex ratio. 'When we are scared about own lives, how are we are going to protect our daughters and ensure that they stay safe and alive? In a way, the birth of a daughter shows us how helpless and vulnerable we are.'

~

I first met 13-year-old Janvi on 19 April 2014. Just three days earlier, she had left their two-room house in Bhagana, left Haryana and come to New Delhi for the first time in her life. Her parents, siblings and 90 other Dhanuk families travelled with her to Delhi. Sushma, Leela and Meena, her three friends who were also assaulted the same night she was, travelled with her to Delhi. On 16 April 2014, they pitched a tent at Jantar Mantar and sat down to protest.

The night of 19 April was fiercely hot. Janvi and the clan came to Jawaharlal Nehru University (JNU) that night because students had organized an awareness and solidarity meeting to support the cause of the Dalits of Bhagana. Sushma, Leela, Meena and Janvi entered the mess of Sutlej hostel at 10 pm. All four girls had covered their faces with cotton dupattas.

Of the four, Janvi was physically the smallest. She looked fragile and sleepy. She curled her legs up on a bench and sat quietly during the whole meeting. I tried to start a conversation. She responded with silence.

I met Janvi again 10 days later that month. At Jantar Mantar, the Bhagana Dalits were to organize their first candlelight protest march that evening. This time too, Janvi met my overtures with silence. For most of the day, she didn't speak to anyone. At any given time, the shamiana at the camp only covered a fraction of the 90 families who had migrated with her from Bhagana. Janvi slept through the afternoon to deal with the heat. She woke up early evening and washed her face. For a moment it was as if she was getting ready like children all over the city who were setting out to play in the cooler evening hours. But soon enough she covered her face again with her dupatta and prepared herself for the candlelight protest march. All around us were Dalit rights activists, members of OBC student forums and politicians from Haryana such as Vedpal Tanwar. That evening I saw her, a thin little girl with a candle in her hands, walking from her tent on Jantar Mantar Road towards the Parliament Street police station. The police barricades stopped the march barely 800 metres away from where it started.

In June, I went to Jantar Mantar thrice to see her. Most of the time she was surrounded by her mother and other women from her community. She largely stayed silent when I spoke to the adults. On one occasion in June, during a fleeting conversation, she gave me a very brief account of the events of the night of the crime in an indifferent tone. An account she was now, three months later, habituated to repeating to journalists.

In mid-July of 2014, Janvi and I had our first long conversation, almost four months after we first met. Clouds covered the Delhi sky but there was no trace of rain. Now the crowd comprised of NGOs, numerous Delhi-based organizations that had espoused the 'Dalit cause' in April, social activists and media crews had disappeared. The politicians who had been around till June, like Tanwar, were absent. The camp, which had bustled with activity and force, now only had 20 people. Most of the 90 families were back at

the Hisar protest camp. The numerous protest posters that had
been pinned on the tent were replaced by one big 'Bhagana
Kand Sangharsh Samiti' banner. Bagoriya and Jagdeesh Kajala
were now leading the fight under the new banner. Bagoriya
and Kajala had also led the 2012 protest migration of Dalits
from Bhagana village. They were among the first in Bhagana
village to protest against the unjust land distribution practices
and everyday exploitation of Dalits by land-owning Jats.
Bagoriya, in his 50s, is a Kumbhar by caste. He has faced
discrimination all his life in Bhagana and grew up to become
a rebel. He lives in a cheap rented house on the outskirts of
Hisar and works full-time for the Bhagana Dalit cause. Kajala
is young, just 25. A Chamar by caste, he and his family faced
severe humiliation after the Jats boycotted them. A wall
came up in front of Kajala's house, cutting them off from the
rest of the village. He says they were all so scared of being
attacked at night that they chose to sleep indoors under the
thin protection of quilts even in the unbearable summer heat.
Kajala once played and practiced on the disputed playground,
keen to build a physique that would get him a job in the police
or the army. Now he too is a full-time activist of the Bhagana
Kand Sangharsh Samiti and wants to 'fight till the end'.

Kajala says, 'This was our first protest in Delhi and the
capital's media and NGO circle have taught us a lesson that
we will never forget. We have been protesting at the Haryana
mini-secretariat for two years now but never faced such
politics. People came here to get their pictures clicked with
the Haryana rape victims, to hijack the issue, for money and
for publicity. We came here with the hope that our sisters
would get justice like Nirbhaya got. But now we understand
that village Dalits are only meant to be used and then left.'

As we are talking I spot Janvi, dressed in a pink salwar

and a yellow kurta, running around the camp, chasing little children from her clan. She smiles mildly at me.

Soon after the families began their protest at Jantar Mantar, the Haryana Department of Social Justice and Empowerment announced that each of the four families would be given Rs 1.2 lakh compensation. The money has not made a dent in the determination of the families who know they are fighting for a life of dignity, a life without fear, in which they know their neighbours cannot treat their daughters like animals.

Bagoriya is despairing, 'The case is slipping away from our hands every day. One of the accused is now out on bail and we've failed to convince the court and police to record fresh statements of all four girls under Section 164 of the CrPC in a fearless environment and to add supplementary charges against Bhagana village sarpanch Rakesh Panghal and his aides in the FIR. Forget everything, we still have an FIR documenting the complaint of only the eldest girl Meena!'

The tent is, for all purposes, sex-segregated. In the women's section, a poster of B.R. Ambedkar is propped up on a plastic chair. Children are playing as if they are not far from home, living on a sidewalk. Two women are washing utensils near the road. I spot Janvi again, walking at a fast pace clutching a new pack of soap and a few clothes. I asked Janvi's mother Bhagmati if her daughter would talk to me for a few minutes. She agreed.

While Bhagmati was preparing evening chai for the family, Sushma and Leela were cutting vegetables for dinner. Janvi arrived and sat down in front of me on the plastic sheet on the ground. She still looked fragile, but not exhausted. Under the green dupatta that covered her head I saw large streaks of white hair. When I asked Bhagmati who was pouring tea into steel tumblers, she said, 'I don't know why but a lot of her hair has always been white. Deficiency or disease, we don't know.' Janvi, who has been playing with the cake of soap in her hands, is restless. She smiles and asks politely, 'Didi, can you come tomorrow? I have to wash my clothes now.'

When I arrive at Jantar Mantar the next day it's raining. With only 12–15 family members sitting around, the protest camp seems even more deserted. The rain has ended the sex-segregation. Men and women have converged into a small dry patch below the cloth tent. All the bedding, clothes, rations and grains are in a heap in this patch. Janvi, Sushma, Leela and their mothers are sleeping on the pile of bedding. Meena has gone back to Hisar to attend her cousin's wedding—the same one Reetika had returned to the village for. All around the protest tent, rainwater collects in pools.

In a little while, Janvi and the others wake up. She adjusts her green dupatta and smiles in greeting. They make space for me and we sit watching the rain. And that evening for the first time, Janvi goes into a detailed description of events of the night of 23 March 2014 as Sushma and Leela look on.

Janvi's Narrative: 'My exams were going on and that evening I was trying to study. Then around 8 pm, I stepped out of my house to pee. Meena, Sushma and Leela used to live in my neighbourhood and we often used to go pee together. That night also, all four of us stepped out and just at a little distance from their houses, a big white vehicle stopped in front of us. There were five Jat boys in that car. I immediately recognized three of them. They were from our village. They called out to Meena. She refused to go and they started pulling her inside. When we tried to stop them, they pulled all of us into the car. They put a cloth in front of our mouths. It had a strange cold smell. I began losing my consciousness slowly soon after. I was carried to the fields by the boys. I remember someone touching my body; I felt the hurt and the changing weight of bodies over me. But I was not in a position to resist, to shout or to even open my eyes properly. It was hazy and then I completely blacked out.

'When I woke up the next morning, Meena, Sushma and Leela were lying next to me. I remember when I first tried to get up, my arms and stomach started aching a lot. I felt a very heavy and piercing pain below my stomach as if somebody was hammering a nail on a wall. I also felt hurt on my cheeks, jaw-line, scalp, shoulders and legs. I was at a railway station (later I realized we were at Bhatinda station), I was so baffled and scared by what might have happened to me that I started crying.'

As Janvi and the girls speak we realize a handful of men passing by in the rain have stopped and are trying to overhear our conversation. I ask the men to leave. Seventeen-year-old Sushma says, 'By now, we knew that we were raped. We could just feel it in our bodies. We were in pain and were still feeling dizzy. Even the Punjabi people standing around us realized that something terrible had happened to us. We understood that we were far away from our village, in Punjab now. We tried to ask them how we could reach home, but we did not understand each other's language. They spoke Punjabi and we talked in Haryanvi.'

A detail they barely registered at the time was this. Meena had woken up to find a phone tucked into the neckline of her kurta. 'We didn't know what to do. But a few hours later, we saw our fathers with the sarpanch coming towards us.'

How did their fathers know where the girls were? This has been one of the strangest, most terrifying aspects of the case.

On the night of 23 March 2014, the fathers of all four girls went to the sarpanch's house, as they do in all emergencies, and told him that their daughters were missing. As Janvi's father Lakshman told me later, 'He asked us to drop the idea of going to the police and told us to wait till morning. He said that our daughters would return the next morning, and going to the police would bring us a bad name. We were restless, but we went back home. All of us went to him again the next morning. This time he told us that he knew the exact location of our girls. After that, he hired a big car and took all of us to Bhatinda. He took us to our girls who were sitting at Bhatinda railway station.' Sarpanch Rakesh Panghal later told me that Sumit Panghal, the prime accused, had told him the exact location of the girls over the phone.

They travelled back together—the girls, their fathers, the sarpanch and his uncle Virendra. In the car, the girls cried quietly. They were still in pain, dizzy and sleepy. They reached Hisar around 10 pm on 24 March. In Hisar, the girls say, the sarpanch stopped the car at a restaurant. He made the four girls eat on the first floor of the restaurant. At this point, Leela in a tight angry voice describes the first of the incidents that indicated to the girls that their troubles were not over. 'While our fathers were eating downstairs, he came up and threatened us. He said that if we took his or any of his family members' or Jat community members' names in this incident or dared to complaint about what had happened to us, he would kill us immediately. He also said that he would kill our parents and that he could very easily destroy our families at any time.'

For the rest of the week, the girls and I talk. On one of those days, we turn to what happened when they reached home. Sushma says, 'At home, our fathers were very worried because they wanted to file a complaint with the police and at the same time they also feared a brutal backlash from the angry Jats. Had this happened to just one of us, they would have never gone to the police. But since we were four girls from different families, all the Dhanuk men from our village collectively decided that we would file an FIR. The sarpanch and his men tried their best to stop us from filing a case. On the morning of 25 March, we somehow reached Hisar's Sadar police station with our fathers,' says Sushma. The Hisar police sent all four girls to a local government hospital for medical examination.

Janvi remembers that day as one of the most painful days of her life, no less than the crime she survived on the night of 23 March. 'That day, we reached the hospital at 10 am in the morning and were asked to sit on a bench before the tests began. The whole morning passed, then afternoon passed and then evening passed and nothing happened. We kept on sitting there hungry, sleepy and silently crying in pain. But no doctor came.' Meena was the first to be examined—at 11.30 that night. 'I was examined post-midnight. I was already sleepy and in tears when I went to the doctor.'

After delaying the girls' medical examination for a whole day, the police then did a shocking thing. They insisted on taking the girls' statements in front of a magistrate right then in the middle of the night—a procedure usually followed only if a victim is on their deathbed.

Janvi says, 'Our statements were recorded between 1.30 am and 3 am. I don't clearly remember what I said in my statement because I was very tired, too hungry and sleepy to understand anything. My whole body was aching, I was in a state of great pain. Around 3.30 am, the cops left us outside the magistrate's home and went away. It was raining heavily and I was crying. I don't know how our fathers brought us to the protest camp situated in front of Hisar's mini-secretariat where our people were. I reached the camp and immediately fell asleep on the ground.'

An FIR was filed on 25 March at the Sadar police station of Hisar against Sumit Panghal, Lalit Panghal, Sandeep Panghal and two unknown persons. By 1 April, police arrested the three named and accused along with two more—a man named Parmal and a juvenile who was later released on bail. The five Jat boys from Bhagana were booked under Sections 363, 366, 366A, 376, 120B and 328 of the Indian Penal Code. Besides, charges were also leveled under the Protection of Children from Sexual Offences Act, 2012 and the Scheduled Caste and Scheduled Tribes (Prevention of Atrocities) Act, 1989. The FIR counts 18-year-old Meena as the only victim of the Bhagana gang-rape. Along with the FIR, the statements recorded under Section 164 of the CrPC also say that all the girls apart from Meena were not conscious, and do not know what happened to them on the night of 23 March. The medical examinations of all four girls confirmed rape.

This is why for months the Bhagana Kand Sangharsh Samiti has been demanding that the statements of all four girls should be recorded afresh in a fearless, healthy environment. And that the complaints of the other three girls should be added to the FIR.

### Janvi's lawyer

On July 21, the parents of three of the four girls were sitting inside Room No. 434 of the lawyers' area situated in the Hisar mini-secretariat. They had woken up at 3 am at their Jantar Mantar camp. Then they walked to Kashmiri Gate and got on the cheapest bus available to reach Hisar. The girls' case was listed for hearing that day in the Haryana trial court.

When I arrived in the morning, the families were sitting in the protest camp outside the mini-secretariat. Over the last two years some of the families have made do at the camp. Others have started living in small rented rooms in Hisar. The families from the Chamar and Khanti communities who have been in Hisar for two years helped the Dhanuk families find daily wage work and cheap places to live. All of them take turns to sit at the Hisar protest site.

Later in the lawyer's chamber, the girls' lawyer Jitendra Khush told the parents about recent developments in the case. None of it was good news.

On 8 July 2014, Jitendra Khush and his senior Ram Niwas had filed an application in the Hisar court for a re-investigation, arguing that the Haryana police had been biased and negligent. They also argued that the magistrate had violated the provisions of Section 164 (CrPC) by not giving the girls the mandatory warning that they only had to make the statement if they felt unafraid and comfortable, that there was no compulsion for them to make it right then in the middle of the night. Despite the victims mentioning that they knew three of the assailants, the magistrate did not ask the girls to identify them, nor did he mention any names in the recorded statement.

The lawyers' application further argued that there was a caste bias on the part of the authorities towards the Dalit girls. Despite corroborating the statements of the victims and their families who accused sarpanch Rakesh Panghal and his uncle Virendra of conspiring in the abduction and gang-rape of the victims, the police had not filed any charges against them. Moreover, the application questioned the Haryana police for trying to discredit the allegations of the survivors by dropping Section 328 of the IPC from the charge-sheet.

In a written reply that had arrived the morning of 21 July 2014, the Haryana police had categorically denied all charges and asserted that the investigation was done properly. And brought in a shocking new red herring. In their response, the police said they had looked at the 'call details of the victims'. To sum up, they found a phone which they say belonged to one of the girls. They say that the GPS data indicated that before Bhatinda railway station, the phone was last located at a place called Sathrod. The police argued that the girls would have had to change two trains to reach Bhatinda, and this could not have been possible if they were unconscious. The police also say that the girls' medical reports do not prove the presence of any sedatives (considering the medical examination was done almost two full days after their abduction, this is unsurprising).

I have been here before with police massaging the evidence of difficult sexual violence cases into a story of romance, youthful high spirits or honour killings, thus shifting the blame to the victim or the victim's family. As I was following the story of the girls of Bhagana, another gang-rape case I had reported on, one that had ended in murder, was taking that direction in Uttar Pradesh.

I asked Khush how the mobile phone location of one girl confirmed the presence of other three with her. And at a more fundamental level, where had the police found this phone and how had they established that it belonged to the girls?

Khush was firm. 'But the police are right. The eldest girl had a phone! Don't you see the call records? 99.9 per cent rape cases here are like that only. They are all consensual,' he added. The parents were puzzled and quiet. Part of it was that they had trouble following non-Haryanvi Hindi.

I asked why he didn't believe his own client, and how he could say that most rapes in Haryana were consensual. 'So what do you think about those numerous cases in which women file a complaint after one or two years of being raped? And sometimes they say that they were being raped continuously for months? How is it possible? I think first they form relations with consent and then file charges of rape later if they feel cheated or neglected. And in this case, call records show that the girls went on their own.'

Back in Delhi, a team of lawyers from the non-profit group Human Rights Law Network (HRLN) has been fighting a separate case in the Supreme Court for the compensation and proper rehabilitation of the Bhagana Dalits. They believe that the gang-rape is a new extension in crimes against Dalits in that region.

I went to see the Hisar SP, Vikas Dhankar, who also has an office in the mini-secretariat. He emphasized that they have been diligent in their investigations. And in an unbiased manner, of course. With a distressed expression, he said, 'Lower caste? You should know that these lower caste people are now coming out and filing complaints against the atrocities happening to them. The situation is not like how it used to be years ago. And I tell you, wait for the next 10 years. This whole caste system will get finished itself. You see, with all these inter-caste marriages happening around, how can caste survive?'

~

In Jat-dominated parts of Bhagana village I meet sarpanch Rakesh Panghal. A clean cement road that runs past many big houses of influential Jats leads to Panghal's double-storeyed home in the best part of the village. I am made to sit in a small outer room of the house, where the sarpanch is sitting with an elderly family member who is reading a newspaper and smoking a hookah. Panghal himself is in his late 30s, and when I meet him, he is wearing a golden and cream kurta and white pajamas, constantly answering calls and checking his smartphone.

As I enter his house, he says he's already heard information that a journalist had entered the Dalit tola. He instructs me to switch off my tape recorder and refuses to be photographed. 'If you still want a picture, I will send you a good one on WhatsApp. I am not looking nice right now.' Categorically denying all allegations about his involvement in the gang-rape of the four Dalit girls, he says, 'They are absolutely lying because they want to frame us so that they can get money from the government for free. Don't you know that the girls got compensation of Rs 1.2 lakh each from the government? Now, I will tell you tell what actually happened. On that night, these girls fed their parents sedatives and then came out of their homes at around 11 pm. The eldest one, Meena, was having an affair with Sumit. So she called him and told him that all four of them have come out and that he should come to pick them up. Sumit, being a *sanskari* boy, said no. They again called and kept on pleading with him. He was concerned about the girls as it was around midnight by then. So he took out his motorcycle and walked with it for a kilometre so that he didn't wake his family. He went to the girls, made them sit on his motorbike and took them to nearby fields. Then he kept on trying to convince the girls to go back home. But they wouldn't listen. Then two of his friends who were returning from a wedding joined them. Sumit asked them to drop the girls to the railway station and he came back home quietly. After that, the whole night he kept on calling the girls and asking them to come back home. But they had boarded the train to Bhatinda on their own. And they are doing all this drama. But I am sure that we will win in the court, you just see. We have already got one of the accused out on bail since he is a juvenile. All the other boys will also come out very soon, you just see.'

In Bhagana's Dalit tola, I meet Sheela—Meena's mother. She has just returned from the wedding in her family and is soon leaving again to join the other survivors and their families at Jantar Mantar. Her daughter is, according to the authorities, the only victim, but just barely, given that the police are now pushing the consensual theory.

I mention the call details present in the chargesheet to Sheela and ask her if her daughter had a phone. She says, 'No, none of them ever had any phone. In fact, the girls told us that the accused had left a phone in Meena's clothes. She found that phone with her when she woke up on the Bhatinda railway station. Later that night, Rakesh Panghal and Virendra threatened the girls on their way back to Bhagana. The sarpanch said that if they dared to complain and take the name of any Jat, then he would kill them and destroy all of us. He knew about the phone and immediately snatched it away from the girls. Now, the phone is all a drama to distract the case and an attempt to malign my daughters. They all want to save the accused. Because they are Jats and the police and lawyers and judges... all are upper-caste people. Sometimes I feel so hopeless and I feel that we will never get justice.'

~

It's a humid mid-July afternoon and the day-off bell has just rung at the primary government school of Bhagana where Janvi and all other girls of the village study. Small girls dressed in green cotton salwars and checked green kurtas are running toward their homes. Inside the building of the Government Primary and Middle School, Bhagana, Hisar, I meet senior

teacher Anita Banda who travels from Hisar town every day
to teach in this school of 250 children. She remembers Janvi,
Sushma, Leela and Meena. She says, 'They were all decent in
studies but it would be an overstatement to say that if given
a chance to study further, they could bring revolutionary
changes in their own lives. The reason is that they are already
groomed and conditioned in a way to accept subjugation and
violence as a part of their lives.'

I think of the four girls and their clan sitting on the street
in Delhi, and I feel that Anita is wrong. The girls and their
families are not the ones conditioned to accept violence. It's
the 'upper-caste' families that believe that Dalit families will
accept violence forever.

Banda continues, 'The lives of lower-caste girls follow a
pattern here which is very difficult to break. Men are usually
drunk and useless. Mothers work on the fields and these
young girls have to cook and do all household work from
a very young age. And as soon as they reach Class 5, their
parents start pulling them out of schools to marry them off.
I personally beg many mothers to let their daughters at least
study until Class 10, but lower-caste women rarely agree.
They are too scared to let their daughters come to school every
day. And I can completely understand their fear. I myself face
harassment on my way back home, what assurance can I give
these mothers?'

Sushma's mother Reshma told me another day, 'Jat boys
tease our girls day and night. We can't let them step out of our
homes. We can't send them to school once they start growing
up. Schoolteachers say that they are responsible for the safety
of girls only inside the school building and if something
happens to our girls on their way home, they can't help it. Jat
boys hover around the school gates, chase and molest Dalit

girls on their way back from school. So nobody in our families wants girls to go to school. Daughters of Dalits are the easiest targets for Jat boys. And since the courts, police, government and administration... everything is on their side, we prefer to keep our girls inside our homes. You say that we should keep our fight going, but you tell me, who helped us? We are sitting at Jantar Mantar, just one more forgotten story. I don't have any hope for justice now.'

At Jantar Mantar on one of my visits I meet Suhaana, Bagoriya's 18-year-old daughter. She is the first Dalit girl in the village to go to a Delhi college. She is wearing a purple cotton salwar kameez, and her oiled hair is woven into tight, long braids. But strikingly, unlike all other girls in the camp, her head is not covered with her dupatta, which lies on her shoulders. She remembers what it was like to study at the government school in Bhagana. 'How will you study if your classmates and most teachers call you by shouting out your caste name and then your father's name? The environment at schools in Bhagana is exceptionally hostile for lower-caste girls. For example, when I started getting good marks, teachers started humiliating me and students started abusing me verbally. One teacher always gave me less marks to ensure that a lower-caste girl did not end up coming first in a class full of Jat children.'

'What are Jat girls like?' I ask Janvi. She says, 'Jat girls can do anything. They can go to school without fear; they can play on the playground and roam around the village freely. Most of them study in the village's private school because Jats are rich. This private school also had a special sports teacher for girls! At times, I have also seen a few Jat girls wearing shirt-pant in our village while I have to ensure that the dupatta never falls off my head. They also put dupattas on their heads, but they can wear other outfits too. Jat girls even go out for studies. Most of them go to college in Hisar and even in Delhi while I have to struggle even to continue my Class 5 education. And the biggest difference is that Jat girls are respected in the village. The same Jat boys who molest us every day don't dare to tease or molest Jat girls. My mother always says this disparity is because Jat men believe that Dalit girls are born to service them and they have every right to molest and rape us.'

~

Back in Jantar Mantar, Janvi is somehow still Janvi. The sun has dipped below the horizon and by now Janvi is very hungry. She grabs a fistful of raw rice from a bag. Besides raw rice, Janvi loves eating gulab jamuns. And watching the Hindi television serial *Choti Bahu*. When I tell her that raw rice might give her a stomach ache, she smiles and says, 'I have been eating raw rice for years now. I eat raw rice when I feel hungry and there is no cooked food. I don't like to cook that much. Though, I have to cook when mother tells me to. But I prefer raw rice to cooked rice.'

Her mother cried a little when she was born. Her teacher doesn't think she can make it. But Janvi giggles, squashing any doubts, and says, 'I will study for my Class 5 exams again. I will study further. Sushma will become a policewoman, Leela will become a doctor and I will become a lawyer. Then no one would dare to trouble us and we would be able to help each other.' But she isn't done yet. 'I want to become a lawyer so that I can help girls get quick justice. But I don't know if I will get a chance to study or not.'

Janvi's moment of great happiness and inspiration came about in an unexpected way. In 2012, 16-year-old Nazia—a Dalit girl who lived in Dabra, a village 15 kilometres away from Bhagana—was on her way to her uncle's house. She was kidnapped by a group of 12 Jat men. She was sedated and gang-raped. Days later, when she told her parents what happened, her father tried to raise the issue in the village. The accused is said to have responded with the threat that Nazia's rape had been recorded on his phone and circulated the clip in the village. Nazia's father committed suicide that week.

Dalit women activists agitated until the accused were arrested. Though many Dalit parents in Dabra were terrified and stopped sending their girls to school and college, Nazia did not give up. Since her father's death, Nazia has been bravely fighting a court case against her rapists. In May 2014, two weeks after the Bhagana families came to Jantar Mantar, the Hisar trial court delivered its verdict in the Dabra gang-rape case and sentenced four of the accused to life imprisonment.

As happy as the verdict had made her, Janvi was even more impressed by the way Nazia has been conducting her life for the past two years. 'Do you know, Nazia came to Jantar Mantar to meet us and to show her support in a candlelight march! She was very happy. She will be going to college soon. She had also learned computers. And she also goes to a dance class! She said she'll ensure that all her rapists are punished. I was so inspired by her. I just can't forget meeting her. I want to become strong and happy like Nazia. I also want to study, learn computers and go to a dance class.'

It's May 2014 and the Bhagana case is being heard in the Hisar trial court. The girls are giving their statements. Janvi is squashing any thought that the case will get dismissed. 'I want my rapists to be punished and then I want to settle with my family in some other village and study. I will never go back to Bhagana. I don't want to remember anything about Bhagana now because it only gives me more pain. I think even in this rain and mud, I am better under this open tent in Jantar Mantar than in those humiliating and torturous lanes of Bhagana, where boys mock me when I try to go to school.'

## Postscript

In August 2015, around one year after I reported this story, the Hisar trial court acquitted all four accused citing lack of evidence in the matter to convict them. The trial of the fifth juvenile accused was then pending with a juvenile court in the state. I went to meet Jagdeesh Kajala again at Jantar Mantar after the verdict. He told me that Janvi came out as the bravest among all and stood by her statements till the end in court. Around the same time, 100 Dalit families from Bhagana converted to Islam in a ceremony at Jantar Mantar. Kajala told me that they converted to escape the humiliation of being Dalit under the Hindu caste system and they were left completely hopeless after their four years of fruitless struggle.

# 7

# On Sale—Trafficking Girls

### Story of four tribal girls divided by geography but united by fate

THE STORY OF THE LIVES OF KAJRI, SAAVNI AND SUGANDHI started in the Bhaisdehi tehsil of the Betul district of Madhya Pradesh. They were born in the lap of the picturesque Satpura forest range and grew up playing on the banks of the Purna river, a tributary of Tapti originating from Bhaisdehi. Betul is a predominantly tribal district and more than 90 per cent of its Bhaisdehi block's population constitutes of Scheduled Tribes. Though Bhaisdehi has a significant mix of both Korku and Gond tribals—the two streams of tribal adivasis found in the district—all three girls were born in Gond families.

These three girls entered my life in October 2011—the time when I made my first visit to their huts in their villages. At the time of my visit, both Kajri and Saavni were 12-year-old kids while Sugandhi was 19 and married. Kajri and Saavni were born in Gwadidana village while Sugandhi was born and raised in a village named Pandari. Due to their common Gond tribe background, all of them knew each other. While Kajri and Saavni were practically neighbours, Sugandhi's house in nearby Pandri village was also close by.

The girls knew of Mahadev Hills, one of the highest mountain points in the Satpura forest range falling in the Bhaisdehi tehsil. And like every Gond child, they knew of the vastness of the Satpura forests in real terms. While the rest of India often gets to know about this legendry Central Indian forest range by Hindi writer Bhawani Prasad Mishra's popular poem 'Satpura ke Ghane Jangal' taught in schools, Gond children know and understand the Satpura like their own courtyard. These three girls also knew routes to sneak in and out of the forests. They had knowledge of sweet fruits and poisonous plants. They could also catch the sounds of the footsteps of any dangerous wild animal. They knew how to live with nature and how to protect themselves from wild animals.

But they were not taught to protect themselves from humans.

∽

It's October of 2011 and I am travelling from Betul's district headquarters to Bhaisdehi tehsil. I can feel the winter mist in the air. The two-hour drive to Bhaisdehi is through lush green landscape and hilly rising-and-falling roads. In the car, I look at the passport size pictures of these girls for the first time. With their deep speaking eyes, they all look like flowers.

In February 2011, they were trafficked and sold in the neighbouring Rajasthan state for money. The three-layered network of traffickers involved in selling these girls included Gond tribals from their own villages. People they knew and trusted, including one Gond woman named Suman who was Kajri and Saavni's neighbour in their village.

Today, modern slavery and human trafficking ranks as the second largest 'business' crime which includes 'selling and buying of human beings'.

Spread across large parts of India, the narrative of trafficking of girls covered in this chapter starts from the Satpura forest range of Madhya Pradesh and takes you through the tea gardens of upper Assam via Delhi and Rajasthan. Although reported over a period of three years across four Indian states, this investigation only gives a glimpse into the massive inter-state trafficking networks active throughout India, modus operandi of these networks and the vicious circle of slavery and exploitation in which the trafficked victims get trapped.

## The morning the girls went missing

On the morning of 18 February 2011, Kajri got dressed in her school uniform, took her school bag on her shoulders and stepped out of her house for school. For her, it was a regular school day. Her 38-year-old mother Jhallo Bai remembers waving goodbye to her. Her neighbours remember her walking towards the school. But that was the last time when anyone in the small tribal hamlet of Gwadidana village had seen her. She mysteriously went missing that morning.

Dressed in a cotton sari, her frail-looking mother takes me inside her one room mud hut. There is nothing in this house made of mud and hay except a few utensils and a sleeping mat. But the house is remarkably clean. Jhallo Bai points towards a corner in the house and says, 'She used to sleep here. We slept together at this spot the night before she went missing. She was a very good girl. Very simple child. Would go to school and straight come back home. Often she would help me in household chores and would never trouble me.' Silent tears are flowing down Jhallo Bai's face as she speaks.

The expression of her grief was quiet yet piercing. I remember her blank eyes lost in an eternal gaze.

The family lives in abject poverty, often struggling to make ends meet. After a couple of minutes, the mother looks at me and adds, 'We looked for her for three–four months but couldn't find any trace of her anywhere. Then we had to come back to our routine. We are very poor and we still have mouths to feed in the family. So her father and I have to go to the fields to work. That is why we couldn't continue searching for her.'

Saavni's hut is situated less than a kilometre away from Kajri's. I walk across vegetable plantation patches to reach Saavni's hut. Her mother Munni Bai is cooking chapatis on an open chulah. The hut has a low ceiling, a roof of hay and its walls are built with bamboo sticks. This house also has nothing except cooking utensils and a mat to sleep on.

Saavni's maternal grandfather Shaymu Gondi is there too. Showing a passport size photo of the child he says, 'She went missing the same day as Kajri—on 18 February 2011. I remember that morning when she was going to school, I had told her to come back straight home as soon as her classes get over. I and her mother were planning to go to market that day. *Maine kaha tere liye boonde aur pairpatti laaunga beti* (I told her that I will bring new earrings and anklets for her from the market), and she must come early. I went to the market and bought these little trinkets for her but she didn't return home that day.' The 65-year-old man starts crying holding the picture of Saavni in his hands.

Saavni's mother Munni Bai is still surprised by the fact that her child went missing. Wiping her forehead with her printed orange sari she says, 'I never stepped out of my block area in my entire life. For many weeks, I couldn't believe that my daughter is missing. I would keep thinking of her whereabouts, continue to get worried day in and day out. I don't remember sleeping, eating or even working peacefully since the day she disappeared.'

The dots of Kajri and Saavni's disappearance match with the third missing girl. Sugandhi of the neighbouring Pandri village. Nineteen-year-old Sugandhi also went missing on the same day. And this puzzle of the sudden disappearance of three tribal girls from a sleepy block of this nondescript district was solved only after Sugandhi somehow managed to escape and returned to her village on 5 September 2011.

~

I meet Sughandi at her residence in Pandri village. It has been just one month since her return.

Sugandhi and her mother Santo Bai have been sitting in the courtyard of their one-room house. As I reach, I see food lying around on the floor. The stressed mother was holding Sugandhi in her lap and trying to comfort her. Dressed in a printed old sari, Sugandhi looked sick, depressed and lost.

'She has been vomiting from the day she arrived. Refuses to eat anything. I went to the market and bought jalebi for her. Because whatever may happen, she would never refuse jalebi. This has been her favourite thing to eat since she was a kid. But today she is not eating even that,' Santo Bai says. She informs me that Sugandhi is now three months pregnant.

The mother kept running her fingers across Sugandhi's dry fizzy hair to comfort her. But comfort was far away from Sugandhi's eyes.

After a long spell of motionlessness she finally turns towards me on her own. I hold her hand in mine, trying to comfort her. There is no one else in the courtyard now except Santo, Sugandi and me; I requested few neighbours hanging around to leave. At this point, Sughandi says that she wants to tell her story. I quietly nod.

'My mother got me married to Motu Dhruve last year. But he left for Gujarat in search of labour work and never returned. He did not even call and we lost all contact with him. I felt lonely and unhappy in my in-laws' village. So in February, I came here to my mother's place to spend some days. As soon as I came here, Suman asked me to come with her to visit the nearby Salkalpur fair. Suman lives in Kajri and Saavni's village and we all knew each other. So I agreed to the Salkalpur fair idea.'

As decided, on the morning of 18 February 2011, Sugandhi got dressed and reached the Bhaisdehi bus stand. She was excited because she had never been to Salkalpur and never gone out of her village to see a fair. Suman was already waiting for her at the bus stand with Saavni and Kajri.

'I had no idea that Saavni and Kajri were also coming. They were in their school uniforms. I later got to know that Suman had also allured them with the proposal of going to a fun fair and they had bunked their schools for it. At the bus stand both of them looked very happy. We believed Suman and that we were going to the famous Salkalpur fair. Suman first took us to nearby Balajipuram and from there to Sadar. Here, she took us to the place where trains stop (railway station). We met two people from Selgaon there, Ramesh and his wife Anita. Ramesh bought tickets for all of us except for Anita because she returned from there.'

Selgaon is a village in Bhaisdehi. Sugandhi had seen Ramesh and Anita before but did not know them very well. But she trusted Suman. So they got on a train. It's important to note here that Salkalpur is a popular tourist spot near Dewas in Madhya Pradesh. But it is not connected to a railway station and there is no railway track around. But the girls, who were seeing a train for the first time in their lives, had no clue about this fact. They all trusted their guide Suman.

'When the trains stopped, we realized that we were in a new place called Bina. Kajri and Saavni started crying and wanted to go home. I also started crying. We all wanted to go back home. Then Ramesh said he will take us back home but first we must eat. We were hungry so we ate the *poori-sabzi* he brought for us. But soon after eating the food, everything around me started becoming blurred. The other girls also felt drowsy. We fell asleep. When we woke up we found ourselves in a closed room. Later I figured it was a dharmshala in the Sawai Madhopur district of Rajasthan,' Sugandhi goes on.

'I sensed something was wrong. Saavni and Kajri started crying and screaming as soon as they woke up. We all wanted to go home. But then Ramesh came in and started beating the other two girls. He threatened to kill us if we kept on making noise. Then we were locked up. Next I saw three people who were brought in by Ramesh.'

These three people were three locals named Guddu, Guddi and Teekaram. Now the three-part inter-state trafficking network gets explained in its entirety. Suman makes the first layer by bringing the girls in; Ramesh makes the second layer by acting as a middleman facilitating transit. And the locals who showed up at the dharmshala in the 'delivery city' make for the third layer. The real 'buying and selling' was going to start only now. Sugandhi—who is telling the story is an eyewitness of these 'transactions'.

She further says, 'Teekaram and Guddi came in and looked at all three of us. Then they had a conversation with Ramesh and Suman. Soon after, all of them came in and started beating Kajri. She was threatened and beaten till she surrendered. Then they got her married to a man. Similarly, they got Saavni also married that day. Both the girls were sent away. I don't know where but they were "married off" and sent away. Both

Saavni and Kajri were small kids so it was easy to threaten and control them. I was scared to see all this happen and started crying. I begged in front of Ramesh and Suman. I told them I am already married. That day Suman assured me that I will not be married off. Next day they bought two clothes for me and took me to Sheopur district. I was quiet because Ramesh had threatened to kill me otherwise. In Sheopur, they forced me and got me married to an old man named Kallu Badhai. Kallu would drink and rape me day in and day out. I would cry, plead and beg. One day I fell at his feet and begged him to let me go home. I was howling and cried my heart out. I held his feet and told him about my mother and my village. I begged him to let me go. But he slapped me and said that he had bought me from Suman and Ramesh after paying 45 thousand rupees. He said I was sold to him. After that I used to cry all the time. I felt caged. Then one day I found a chance to slip out of that cage house. I immediately stepped out of the house and started running. I ran and ran and ran and did not look behind. Soon I reached another village. From there I got on a bus. Then I changed buses till I reached my home. When I got here, one of my uncles told us to go to the police and tell them everything. So I went to the police next day and told them everything.'

After Sugandhi's return, Betul police immediately registered a case under the 'immoral trafficking and prevention act' and dispatched its teams to Sawai Madhopur in Rajasthan in search of Saavni and Kajri.

I went to the Scheduled Castes and Scheduled Tribes (SC/ST) superintendent of police (SP)'s office in the district headquarters of Betul to know about the status of the case. The special ST/SC SP, Kiran Kirteka, told me that a case under the 'Immoral Trafficking and Prevention Act' has been registered against nine people, including Suman, Ramesh, Anita, Guddu, Guddi, Teekaram and Kallu Badhai. 'Additional charges of rape and abduction have also been imposed. One more girl has been rescued and three arrests have been made so far. As you know, the sex ratio has been dipping in Rajasthan. In most villages around Sawai Madhopur, men don't find girls to get married to. So these traffickers are trying to make the most of this crisis situation by selling poor tribal girls from Madhya Pradesh in Rajasthan.'

The second girl to be rescued was Saavni. Since she is a minor, she was sent to a government children's home in Bhopal. I managed to see her once in the said children's home. During our brief conversation, she mostly kept silent. Just before the end of our meeting, she said that she had tried to free herself but couldn't succeed. 'I kept crying but no one listened to me. They got me married and did not let me go back to my mother.'

Back in her village in Betul, Saavni's mother Munni Bai is relaxed that her daughter has at last been brought back. 'I used to have bad dreams all the time. I would think if she is alive or dead. Thank god that Sugandhi came back and the police tracked down my daughter after that. Otherwise god knows what those traffickers might have done with my child!' she says with moist eyes.

On the other side, Sugandhi's mother Santo Bai is not thinking of her daughter's future at all. She tells me that she is only worried about Sugandhi's health. 'They trafficked and sold her to someone. My own village people were involved in this whole crime. They are being caught by police. I know god will do justice with my child. And now when she is three months pregnant, what can I say about her future? Who knows if we still have a future? I am not worried about what people might say. I am only worried about her health. Her body aches all the time and she has fever. She keeps crying. All I want is for her to be healthy again.'

As I leave Sugandhi's home, the look in her mother's determined eyes stay with me. I think to myself: Why is this only possible in the comparatively liberal tribal households in India—where parents worry more about their children's health that their so called 'honour'? My respect and belief in the adivasi way of life has increased manifold and somewhere I made a silent prayer in my heart: May the 'city people' learn a thing or two from these people of nature—the adivasis.

Twelve-year-old Kajri has still not returned. But after Sugandhi and Saavni's return, her mother Jhallo Bai looks hopeful. As I say goodbye to her, she says, 'Police brought back the other two girls. Hopefully, my Kajri will also return one day. Will she come back? Tell me, madame. Will she come back?'

'She will, she will,' I say to her.

As I drive out of Betul, my mind keeps going back to the mothers: Jhallo, Santo and Munni. Will their eyes ever leave me?

I don't think so.

## Human trafficking: The new law

Although India has acts like 1956 'The Immoral Traffic (Prevention) Act' to deal with human trafficking but we had no constitutional and legal definition of human trafficking until 2013. In March 2018, human trafficking was defined for the first time in the amended 'Criminal Amended Act, 2013'.

The 'Justice Verma Committee' formed after the December 2012 Delhi gang-rape, dedicated a whole chapter to women trafficking in its recommendations. The report clearly states that minors as well as young girls who are being trafficked across India end up being the victims of sexual as well as financial and emotional exploitation. This includes missing girls and girls who are trafficked after being lured by fake promises of employment and even things like 'a touristy trip to a metro city'.

On the recommendations of the Justice Verma Committee, Section 370 of IPC was amended and Section 370 A— defining human trafficking—was added in it. The section says: 'Whoever, for the purpose of exploitation—a) recruits b) transports c) harbours d) transfers or e) receives a person or persons by using threats or using force or any other form of coercion or by abduction or by practicing fraud or deception or by abuse of power or by inducting, including the giving and receiving of payments or benefits—in order to achieve the consent of any person having control over the person recruited or transported or harboured or transferred or received—is committing the offence of trafficking.'

The new law also states that in case of trafficking, the consent of victim is immaterial. Also, the punishment for this crime is 10 years of rigorous imprisonment. This will extend to life term in case of repeat offenders or for people who have trafficked more than one person or for trafficking minors.

With the Criminal Amended Act (2013) coming into force, it was expected that the graph of trafficking will go down in India. By now, the stringent 2012 POCSO Act (The Protection of Children from Sexual Offences Act) was also in force. But did things improve?

## Women trafficking in Assam

In the summer of 2013, I travelled to the Lakhimpur district
of upper Assam. Situated around 2100 kilometres away from
Delhi, Lakhimpur is a picturesque district of Assam tucked
away at the northwestern tip of the state. It took me more
than 24 hours of travel time spread across a two-hour flight,
an overnight bus journey and multiple taxi trips to reach
Lakhimpur. As I drove closer to the district, I admired the
lush green tea gardens and water-filled paddy fields.

Sandwiched between the mighty Brahmaputra and
Subansiri rivers, Lakhimpur looks like a beautiful happy green
place at first sight. But as I made my way to the interiors of
rural Lakhimpur, a grim cycle of poverty, unemployment and
human trafficking started emerging. With around 40 girls
going missing every month, this district with a population of
roughly 10 lakh Indians is emerging as a new hub of human
trafficking in India.

During my reporting trip to Lakhimpur I discovered a
multi-layered network of illegal placement agencies based in
metro cities like Delhi/Bombay and their nexus with the local
agents who have been luring girls from the district; and how
they are working together to lure young girls into a vicious
circle of exploitation with promises of jobs, money, marriage,
a life in the city or simply a trip to a metro city.

Almost every village in Lakhimpur has its share of stories
of girls who went to Delhi and never returned. I went to 10
villages and spoke to all kinds of families—girls who had
somehow managed to return after facing sexual, physical and
psychological exploitation for years to families of those girls
who are dead to those who are still missing. While some were
pushed into prostitution, others were raped by their employers

or by the owners of placement agencies. And then there was the chamber of endless unpaid household work; most of these girls are forced to spend their lives as unpaid bounded slaves working full time at the houses of the rich urban elite of Indian metros.

A confidential report released by the National Human Rights Commission (NHRC) in response to an RTI filed in July 2012 backs the harrowing tales of these 'missing girls of Lakhimpur'. It confirms that a large number of 10- to 15-year-old girls brought from the Northeast to Delhi and Mumbai are victims of human trafficking. The report says, 'Most of these girls are made to sign papers written in English, which they don't understand. Their pay ranges from 2,200–4,500 rupees. But the entire amount is kept by the placement agencies involved in-between. These agencies are not legally registered and function under the Partnership Act. The girls are not allowed to talk to their parents nor are they given permission to visit any of their relatives in Delhi. Most of these girls also become victims of rape and sexual violence. There is evidence that in most cases the local police are aware of these incidents of trafficking and the plight of these girls.'

Armed with the facts and the NHRC report, I first reached the Lukumpur village of Lakhimpur. Here I was to meet Rajni Khatoon.

Rajni was trafficked to Delhi by a fellow villager in 2009. She was only 15 then. After surviving three years of sexual and labour exploitation, she somehow escaped.

In a couple of minutes I am sitting inside Rajni's one-room house. Rajni and her anxious mother are with me. We are the only people in the house now. Her mother says that she suspected me of being from one of those placement agencies and that she was terrified when she saw me walking towards

her courtyard at first. I had shown my press and other identity
cards to the mother and daughter, told them about myself—
my whereabouts and family etc.—and requested them to share
their story with me.

After a few minutes of silence followed by awkwardness,
both agreed to share their story. The mother started the
conversation and told me that Anita Beg, a local agent from
her village, took her daughter to Delhi first.

Just then we realize that someone is standing outside the
only window of the house and eavesdropping. When we check,
we find a local woman from the neighbourhood snooping. The
mother–daughter duo have to hush her away.

We close all doors and windows of the house. We double-
check to ensure no one is hanging around. Then, after a couple
of minutes have passed and both feel more comfortable, Rajni
starts talking.

'Anita used to live in our neighborhood. She would often
tell me stories about Delhi and would say that she can take
me to Delhi, show me around, and then bring me back to my
village. I asked my mother and she said no. The matter ended
there. But then again one day, Anita came to my house in the
absence of my mother. She said she could take me to Delhi
for a touristy trip. She said other girls were also going with
her. And they will also get paid good money for very little
work. I thought I will tag along, see India Gate and come
back. Anita said she will drop me back home in one or two
days. So I went with her.'

It's clear that Anita told lucrative stories about Delhi to
Rajni but did not tell her that it takes around three days to
reach Delhi from Lakhimpur by land. Rajni imagined that
she would be back from Delhi in either one or two days. But
that was only her imagination.

In Delhi, Rajni was taken to a placement agency in Shakurpur Basti run by Mahesh Gupta. 'I was sent to work as a maid at a bungalow in Punjabi Bagh. I had to work 14 to 16 hours every day in that huge house. I was made to do everything from cooking to cleaning to mopping. I had no access to the outer world and I felt like I was living in a cage. I would cry at night and would think of my mother and our little village house all the time. Whenever I asked to go home, I was told that I couldn't go anywhere for one year. After one full year of daily work, I was sent to Gupta's office again. He didn't pay me anything—not even a single rupee—and sent me to work in a new bungalow in Ahmedabad.'

At this point, Rajni suddenly breaks down into tears. I tell her that we can stop the conversation anytime, whenever she wants. But she drinks a glass of water and continues.

'When I told my new employer that Gupta and the placement agency didn't pay me anything and that I wanted to go home, he gave me 11 thousand rupees in my hand and sent me back to the placement agency. Gupta kept all the money and after two years of bone-breaking forced labour in Delhi and Ahemdabad, he kept two thousand rupees in my hand and put me on a train to my home.'

Rajni was devastated but at least she came back home in 2011. But her ordeal was far from over. Rajni told her family about the hard work she did for two years in Delhi and soon word spread in the village that Rajni got only two thousand rupees for two years of grueling physical work. A local agent named Walson Godra took advantage of the discontent and frustration simmering inside Rajni. He tricked her into believing that he had good contacts with Mahesh Gupta's placement agency and that he was friends with Gupta. 'He started coming to my house every second day and would tell things like—according to market rate I should get at least one lakh rupees for my two years of work. He would say that he will get me my hard-earned money back in my hands and I can come back home immediately. I did not want to go because of my past experience but I also felt violated. I felt angry and cheated. I wanted the money for my hard work. The bad behaviour and abuse that I got while working couldn't be undone but at least I could get paid for my hard work. Walson said that he will fight for my money. So I went against my mother's wishes once again and took the train to Delhi with Walson.'

Instead of going to Mahesh Gupta, Walson took Rajni to another agency in Delhi run by two men named Imran and Mithun. He left Rajni alone at the agency and quickly disappeared.

'I was shocked and scared as hell. I had no money in my hand and I didn't know what to do. When I got Walson called from the agency, he told me that he has left for Assam and would come back soon to take me back. I cried the whole night. The next day, I was told that Walson had sold me off for 10 thousand rupees. I was forced to work at a new bungalow in Rohini. But I ran away from there after a month.'

But Rajni couldn't run away. The agency was informed by her Rohini employers and she was brought back to the placement agency office in the Sakurpur suburb of Delhi. She requested and begged to be sent back home. But nothing changed the circumstances for her.

'Imran and Mithun got very angry with me for trying to run away. There were three other boys present there. Imran and Mithun told them to take me away and 'do whatever they want to do with me'. Mithun threatened me that if I didn't agree to work, he will send me to a worse place—a place so bad I cannot imagine.'

Rajni had high fever that night. The men took her out in a car on the pretext of taking her to a doctor. 'I knew in my heart. Never on earth will they take me to a doctor. But I was too sick, weak and bruised to resist. Everything felt dizzy and blurred. When I woke up I found myself locked in a room. I have no clue where I was. The men—Imran, Mithun and the other three boys—raped me for seven days inside that room. They would say that they were "making up for the losses I had caused them by running away from the Rohini bunglow". After that, in the dead of the eighth night, they left me outside Old Delhi railway station and drove away. I felt that I was dead. I was weak, bleeding and could not make sense of anything. An auto driver standing outside the station helped me and I got on a train to go home somehow.'

~

In this context, I want to mention a reply given by then Union Minister of State for the Development of North Eastern Region, Paban Singh Ghatowar, in 2013's Budget Session of Parliament. While answering a question on trafficking and missing children, Ghatowar agreed that the count of 'missing children' from Lakhimpur 'has been on rise recently'. 'But the police is working to trace them down and many have been found also,' he said. 'We have issued a notice that a complaint should be registered every time a child goes missing.'

Kailash Satyarthi, who runs a child rights NGO in Delhi makes a dark but apt analogy when he says that buying a 'girl' costs less than 'buying a cow or a buffalo' in Assam today. In an interview with this writer, he mentioned the newly amended trafficking laws in the country. 'The Criminal Law (Amendment) Act and multiple decisions given by Supreme Court in the matter of missing and trafficked girls make it mandatory for the police to not only register cases of missing girls but also to probe the functioning of local agents and placement agencies under Sections 370 and 370 (A) of IPC. But it's a fact that traffickers are still shielded by politicians and the police. It's because nobody wants female trafficking to stop. They all profit from it.'

~

Rajni's mother is crying. She hugs her daughter and pats her back trying to comfort her. Then she turns to me and says, 'My daughter faced hell! I hope no mother on earth has to go through the pain that I have gone through. Forget the money, her life was almost gone. And she has not recovered fully yet. Her abdomen still hurts. You are from the city, you know how society is. Our whole village knows what happened with my daughter in Delhi. Now who will marry her? Everywhere we go, people taunt my daughter and pass bad comments. Police did nothing. What are we supposed to do? Is there any justice for poor people in this world? You tell me madame, is there any justice for my daughter?' she shakes my arm and asks.

I have tears rolling down my face now. I hold the rough hard hands of Rajni's mother and hug her. I hug Rajni and request her to take care of herself and to not lose hope. I write the name and phone number of a local human rights lawyer working for the cause of trafficked children on a piece of paper and hand it over to the mother. As I bid goodbye, my heart feels heavy.

Rajni walks me out till the main road of the village and stands there waving her short hand in the air till I drive out of her vision.

I feel a sharp churning pain in my stomach. There are moments in my reporting life, when all I have wanted to do is to howl. I want to scream loudly—so loud that my voice reaches the sky and breaks it apart in two pieces. Instead I cover my face with my scarf and sob. Silently. Because I don't want the driver to know that I am crying. Otherwise he might assume that I am a 'weak woman'. And no good thing happens to 'weak' women in this world.

## Post Script

During this investigation, I spoke to nine human traffickers who revealed that as many as 40 girls go missing every month from the district. They confessed on record to having trafficked around 187 girls to Delhi since 2005. This writer's investigation in the Lakhimpur women trafficking nexus is also part of supporting evidence submitted with a Public Interest Litigation (PIL). This PIL has been filed in the Guwahati High Court to secure justice for the 'missing girls of Lakhimpur'.

# 8

## Hanging from a Mango Tree

### The rape and murder of the Badaun sisters

MOST INDIANS WILL PERHAPS NEVER FORGET THE INFAMOUS image of two minor girls hanging from a mango tree in the Badaun district of Uttar Pradesh in May 2014. The alleged gang-rape and murder of these two Badaun cousins shot India again into the global spotlight for brutality and violence against women. Though violence against women is an everyday thing in India. So much so that there is a sense of creeping normalization towards the dozens of crimes against women reported in newspapers daily. But the case of the Badaun sisters captured people's imagination throughout the world and evoked shock, anger, protests and empathy. One reason behind this outrage was the image of the bodies of these two children hanging from the mango tree—slowly swinging in the burning afternoon winds of a North Indian summer.

As weeks passed by, the alleged rape and murder of the Badaun sisters turned into another blind mystery with no answers to the fundamental question: Who committed the crime and why? But there was a major shift in the course of investigation after the Central Bureau of Investigation (CBI) took over the case in June 2014. The CBI did file its closure report in the matter in December 2014 and the local court rejected the ace investigative agency's report in October 2015. But what happened in between tells you the complex story of the loss of two lives in an Uttar Pradesh village—and how the victims' families were pitched against an intimidating investigative procedure, unforgiving power politics and an active caste war.

I went to Badaun to report this story, first time in June 2014 and the second time in April 2015. The second trip was only a confirmation of what I had reported during my first trip. During my April 2015 visit, the victim's family told me in great detail about their harrowing experiences of going through the CBI investigation. Armed with exclusively scooped official documents and recorded interviews, I have kept all sides of the story in front of the readers in this chapter.

For the sake of maintaining chronology, I have written accounts of my two reporting trips to Badaun in the order in which they happened.

**First reporting trip—June 2014**

If the Ganga hadn't submerged the village of Badam Nagla four years ago, would Kavita and Ragini still be alive today? That is as pointless as asking would Kavita and Ragini be alive today if they had not needed to leave their house at night to pee.

Was it just chance that the girls, barely in their teens, caught the eye of a group of violent, entitled men the night of 27 May 2014? Perhaps. Or were they targets picked in the deliberate way of predatory men? Perhaps. It's difficult to tell. Their stories are becoming increasingly blurred by the name of the district—Badaun.

～

Every year the Ganga and its tributaries swallow a few villages in Badaun. Villages slowly vanish under huge deposits of silt. Four years ago, after a powerful flood, Badam Nagla village in Farrukhabad district was almost entirely submerged. Residents of this small village migrated to nearby villages like Manthpura, Salik ka Nagla, Pattharrani.

Veerpal Yadav, his wife and three sons, were among the handful of families that migrated to Katra Sadatganj from Badam Nagla. His eldest son Avadesh got married in 2013 and has a child. Urvesh, his second son, studied up to high school. Residents of Katra Sadatganj say that his youngest— 24-year-old Pappu Yadav—was the most notorious of the three brothers. 'He used to roam about, do nothing and harass girls,' says 60-year-old Durgpal Shakya, a resident of Katra village. All three Yadav brothers are now arrested for raping and murdering two young girls in Katra Sadatganj, the village that for a month has been known to most Indian newspaper readers and TV viewers as 'Badaun, where the two girls were hanged from a tree'.

All of these villages are situated on the banks of the Ganga. Two small rivers known as Ramganga and Bahugul flow in this region across the adjacent borders of Badaun, Farrukhabad and Shahjahanpur districts. The villages here in the Katri belt (*Katri patti ke gawn*) are largely dominated by people from the Yadav caste and are infamous for crime. The Yadav families grow watermelon on the sandy banks of the Ganga and grow cash crops like tobacco and mint on cultivable land.

It's 30 kilometres from Katra Sadatganj to Manthpura, the village closest to the now-vanished Badam Nagla village. It is where most of Pappu Yadav's clan and former neighbours moved to.

As I get closer to Manthpura, sightings of men on

motorbikes with only a Samajwadi Party flag printed where their number plates should be, driving with two rifles slung on their shoulders, becomes commonplace. The landscape is rough and dotted with ravines, covered in a tall, thick grass locally known as 'patel'. Government primary school buildings stand empty and ruined, yards covered in grass and stagnant water.

The day before, Shahjahanpur-based journalist Vivek Senger, who has been covering crime in the Katri belt for a decade, told me that the whole region had no proper roads, no education, no electricity and no employment opportunities. 'The Katri belt has seen the rise and fall of dacoit gangs like the Kallu Yadav gang and the Najju gang over the years. Most of these gangs developed against the oppression and atrocities of Uttar Pradesh police on common people. Slowly, these Robin Hood-style dacoit gangs got into the business of kidnapping and then, by the end of the 1990s, they turned into small-time semi-urban gangsters.'

When I finally reach Manthpura, alert and curious residents gather around. Many adolescent boys hang about. Children are playing in the lanes. Manthpura is an all-Yadav village and they've all heard of what has happened in Katra Sadatganj. In this watchful atmosphere, I am too nervous to say that I am a reporter, so I introduce myself as a researcher working on the impact of sand silting on riverside villages in the country.

Fifty-year-old Omkar Yadav points his finger towards the river and says, 'That was where Badam Nagla village was situated once. Now the village has vanished in the river. Many families of Badam Nagla now live in Manthpura also.' I see a green marshy area of land now half-submerged in the water. That was where Pappu and his brothers grew up.

After half an hour of hanging around and making small talk, along the Ganga river canal, I meet 60-year-old Munni Devi, a former resident of Badam Nagla. When I mention Veerpal Yadav's family and his sons, she says, 'They left the village long ago. But the boys are innocent, I tell you. What would you do if a girl offers herself to you? It is the girl's fault.' At this point she notices her own teenaged granddaughter hanging about, listening to the conversation. She asks her sternly to go home but the girl only moves out of her line of vision and stays.

Munni Devi continues, 'Men are obviously going to use you if you go and fall on their chests. These lower-caste people do not keep a check on their girls. That girl was also going around with Pappu. It's stupid to first not keep your girls in your control and then to complain that Yadav men raped them. Men are not at fault. These lower-caste girls are all like this.' The men gathered in a crowd around Munni Devi nod their heads in agreement. Omkar says, 'Girls should behave themselves or be ready to face the consequences.' This is presumably what Pappu Yadav and other boys grew up hearing before they moved to Katra Sadatganj.

I think of what crime reporter Vivek Senger told me the previous day, 'Crimes against women have crossed all records in this region. While Yadav women are comparatively safe, the rape and murder of lower-caste women is an everyday thing. There's also a pattern of burning women's faces with acid after killing them. We cover a lot of cases involving unidentifiable corpses of women who have been raped, killed and burnt. The hanging of the two girls from the mango tree? That is just the newest variation.'

~

Nineteen-year-old Phoolan Devi and her 14-year-old brother Pintoo were close to their younger cousins Kavita and Ragini. Pintoo is still in school but his older sister was married last year. Phoolan had just arrived at her parents' home in Badaun for a visit last month when she heard the news that was to rock the whole country. That her cousins had been found dead: hanged from a mango tree.

Small, thin Phoolan, in a pink printed sari, stares at the mud floor of her parents' home while thinking of the two girls. Her brother is dressed in a grey shirt and dark pants. Less composed, he scrubs at the floor to relieve his feelings.

Phoolan says, 'They were my sisters. We all grew up together. We all played, cooked food and embroidered clothes together. Both of them were very good and embroidered new designs on clothes.' Pintoo looks at his sister and murmurs, 'They used to cook very nice food. They would make me dal, roti and nice vegetables. We use to play together. They'd make flowers on handkerchiefs and would show them to me. They were very quick in capturing designs. They made designs on their own dupattas also. You only had to show a design once to Kavita and she'd make it in a few hours. Ragini liked to dress up too. I will always miss most the rakhis that they used to tie on my hand every year.'

Kavita and Ragini had both gone to the same school for a while, the only private school in the village. When Kavita passed Class 8, her parents started looking for a groom and told her that she could resume schooling after marriage. Ragini was in Class 6.

Pintoo's round child face shuts down as he says, 'I cannot forget them hanging from the tree. I try not to but I see them hanging again and again.' This is difficult enough to hear from him, but then his older sister says, 'When I was not married, we use to go to relieve ourselves together.'

The dangers that women in rural India face when going to urinate or defecate in the fields have been widely debated of late. But the dangers they face are not in the dim light of dawn or in the darkness. And it is some of that fear that weighs down Phoolan's voice.

Their uncle Jai Singh says, 'Abduction and rapes of lower-caste girls by Yadavs is very common in this region. Many abductions and rapes have happened in this village. Badaun is a historical bastion of Yadavs. Former Chief Minister Mulayam Singh Yadav's nephew Dharmendra Yadav is the MP from Badaun, and the state government is of the Yadavs. What is a lower-caste Maurya going to achieve by daring to file a complaint against the Yadavs? We are being killed now and will be killed at a much faster pace if we start complaining against the Yadavs. I know many families who have suffered similarly but they never reported the matter as the girls were abandoned after a few hours or a night.'

~

Green grass has already started growing on the emergency helipad specially made for the quick descent and ascent of high-profile politicians into Katra Sadatganj in Badaun district.

A fortnight after the gang-rape and murder of the two young girls, a heavy silence envelopes the Maurya hamlet of Katra Sadatganj village. The camps of media crews have vanished. Gloomy residents can easily be spotted sitting slumped under mango trees. Children with skin so dry from the heat that deep cracks have appeared, wander around a few newly constructed toilets built in the last one year. By now, nobody in the village is even curious about city people coming in with their vehicles and cameras. When they point you to the residence of the two murdered cousins, they are still polite. And the appearance of a jawan (army man), one from the additional forces posted in the village, no longer makes people sit up.

No one is sitting up at the police outpost I pass by. It is 46 degrees celsius this morning. A small clump of mango trees shade this little building at the southernmost tip of Badaun district, around 45 kilometres from the district headquarters. This morning, there are three cots under the trees. Washed shirts, pants and men's undergarments are drying on ropes tied between branches. Shoes, rucksacks, water bottles and used utensils lie on the ground. Two men in track pants and t-shirts are asleep on these cots.

This is the local police outpost of Katra Sadatganj in the Usehat police station area of Badaun district. Chowki in-charge Vijendra Sharma has recently been transferred here. He is the only man in police uniform in the vicinity, and is sprawled on two plastic chairs. When I enter, he sits up and picks up, for company, a newspaper lying on one of the cots. He sits with dignity amidst the flies buzzing over the leftovers in the plates, quiet and a bit reluctant to speak. 'I just came here, I was recently transferred. I know nothing about anything related to this outpost.' This is his comprehensive and justifiable snub to my curiosity.

Nothing seems to have changed in this police outpost since 27 May 2014, when Kavita and Ragini were hanged from a mango tree. This somnolent afternoon, you'd never guess that the Katra Sadatganj police outpost is only 300 metres away from the children's homes. That the entire five-member staff of the outpost, who were present on the night of the crime, have been suspended and two constables have been arrested for 'criminal conspiracy'. That 'Badaun' has in a month's time become shorthand for a certain kind of brutal violence against women and the very particularly Indian aftermath in which justice seems a distant, ridiculous dream.

To reach the house of Sohanlal, the father of one of the murdered girls, I walk through the temporary camps of the special rapid response teams of the Uttar Pradesh provincial armed constabulary (UP-PAC). The CBI has been expected in the village all day.

The girls' fathers, 35-year-old Sohanlal and 30-year-old Jeevanlal, are brothers. They belong to the Maurya caste, also known as 'Shakya' in the region. Mauryas are categorized as an Extremely Backward Class (EBC). Around here, they are mostly vegetable farmers. They are not Dalits, regardless of what all the early reports said and regardless of how neatly that fits a certain narrative, as academic Sruthi Herbert points out in her essay.

Fourteen-year-old Kavita was Jeevanlal and Suneeta's only child. Suneeta had been mother to her ever since Kavita's mother died when she was three years old. Twelve-year-old Ragini was the daughter of Shridevi and Sohanlal. Today, around 30 relatives are sitting in the mud courtyard of Sohanlal's house, braving the scorching heat. It isn't only the heat and the mourning of their terrible loss that is making this clan silent. The family members are also oppressed by fear. In the last 48 hours, there has been a palpable shift in the family's concerns. At first, it seemed like their murdered daughters would get no justice at all. Then it seemed like under the glare of the media, there was a chance that the accused would stand trial. But in the last two days it's been clear to them that there is a steady poisoning of the well, to make it seem that they are the ones who killed their daughters. No, your daughters were not little girls abducted by large, violent men who killed

them. No, you killed your daughters for cavorting with men.
This is the change of tune that the families are hearing.

~

On 7 June 2014, Uttar Pradesh Director-General of Police
Anand Lal Banerjee said at a press conference that the rape of
one of the two girls was not yet confirmed. This was surprising.
And contrary to the original post-mortem report.

The post-mortem of both children had been conducted
in Badaun district headquarters on the night of 28 May by a
team of three government doctors. Dr Rajeev Gupta headed
the panel of three doctors, which also included Dr Pushpa
Pant Tripathi and Dr Awadhesh Kumar. The post-mortem
reports of both girls clearly show and confirm that the girls
were violently raped. Contrary to the ages of 12 and 14
mentioned by victims' parents, the post-mortem reports record
the victims' ages as 14 and 16. The younger child's body was
the first to be examined. After a 50-minute-long (7.05 pm to
7.55 pm) video-recorded examination, the panel commented,
'On perineal examination, bleeding in the form of clotted
blood is seen in and around vaginal orifice. Hematoma present
over hymen and abrasions present around hymen (findings
suggestive of rape).' Later, the video recording of the older
child's post-mortem was conducted in 40 minutes (from 8.35
pm to 9.15 pm). The doctors commented, 'Hymen is bluish
in color. Vaginal tear is present in 5'o'clock position. Vaginal
discharge is present.' Vaginal tears and abrasions around the
hymen are all indicative of forced entry. The doctors' note
in both post-mortem reports says, 'Perineal findings are
suggestive of rape.'

The 28 May post-mortem reports also mention 'asphyxia'
as the girls' immediate cause of death. Asphyxia is the medical

term used to explain the 'acute absence of oxygen which leads to suffocation and death in extreme cases'. The reports also mention that the tongues of the girls were protruding and eyes congested. And that the girls were alive when they were hanged on the mango tree, as asphyxia was caused due to 'ante-mortem' hanging.

After international outrage broke out over the Badaun double murder case, Uttar Pradesh Chief Minister Akhilesh Yadav, sounding distinctly peevish, started blaming the media for not studying rape statistics and for blowing the Badaun double murder out of proportion. Other regressive remarks poured in from all points of the Indian political spectrum. While Maharashtra Home Minister R.R. Patil was quoted saying, 'Even if we provide one policeman per house, we can't stop crime against women,' Madhya Pradesh Home Minister Babulal Gaur felt that rape was a social crime between man and woman. 'It is sometimes right, sometimes wrong,' he said.

Adding fuel to the honour killing rumours, Banerjee had said, 'Of the two victims, one was a lone child. Her father has three brothers who have limited resources. In case she is not alive, then it can benefit others. It (property) can be one of the motives. I am not saying that this is the motive.'

The slander-mongering feels very familiar. I've reported extensively on different cases of rape in Haryana. As in Uttar Pradesh, lower-caste communities face fierce, relentless caste-based oppression in Haryana. And when it comes to rape, Haryana has a habit of declaring it consensual. At all the locations in Haryana I went to, rumors always swirled thickly that the victim had been having an affair with the accused. In some cases, while I interviewed the victim inside, local journalists, villagers and relatives would gather outside. The moment I stepped out I'd get multiple people explaining

earnestly how the girl had a 'loose character' and how the rape
was 'actually consensual'.

In most cases, local policemen would only try to cement
the 'consensus' theory which sometimes forced the victim to
withdraw her statement, took away even her moral assertion
that she had been the victim of a crime and left her with no
hope at all. Some of that was happening in Badaun too. The
media had begun reporting how the girls wanted to go to a
mela that night, had borrowed money to go to a mela, how one
of them used to meet Pappu Yadav regularly. No one I spoke
to across the village knew anything about the mela though.

On my way to Badaun, in the nearest big town of Bareilly,
reporters talked darkly of policemen getting orders from above
to make the case go away. And with the superimposition of
the motives for which middle class, landed Indian families
regularly kill each other—shame and property—on the
families of the Maurya girls, the road to making the case go
away had been laid. By the time I reached Badaun, the honour
killing theory had well and truly muddied the waters.

~

Sohanlal's house consists of two rooms, a small mud hutment
and a mud courtyard. All day the two brothers have spoken
to several non-profit research organizations and advocacy
representatives for many hours. They look exhausted. After
bidding goodbye to the last legal rights activist, Sohanlal
cuddles his orange polythene bag to catch a small nap in the
mud courtyard while Jeevanlal stares at the roof over his head.
Their elder brother Ram Babu tells me that Sohanlal has kept
multiple photocopies of the documents related to the rape
and hanging of his daughter and his niece—whom he loved
like his own daughter—in that orange polythene bag. 'Also,

he has kept many copies of all photographs which show his daughters hanging from the mango tree in that orange bag. He shows the documents and pictures to everyone who comes to meet him. He is so determined to get justice for his daughters that he never leaves this polythene, not even while sleeping.'

While Sohanlal sleeps, I ask Jeevan about the mothers of the murdered girls. He directs me silently towards two women sitting on the other side of the courtyard. They are so still I worry for a bit whether they've fainted in the heat and no one's noticed. The two young women in bright blue saris are mourning with other female relatives of the extended family. When I talk about her daughter, Ragini's mother Shridevi keeps staring at the mud floor. After a few minutes of silence she says without looking at me, 'They were very nice children. My daughters were very good girls. They would help me in household chores, study, cook with me and make embroidery designs on clothes. They ate whatever we gave them, never bothered us like other children do. They were very helpful and obedient children. I am unable to understand why anyone would kill them so brutally?'

Kavita's mother Suneeta begins sobbing. She says, 'They cooked dinner and went out to relieve themselves, like they did every day. When they did not return, men started searching for them all over and we started shouting and wailing in our homes. By morning we were told that our daughters are hanging on the mango trees of Ramnath Chaudhary's orchard. We never imagined that somebody could kill our children so cruelly.'

As Suneeta talks to me, Shridevi suddenly starts sobbing inconsolably. She cries and repeats the first name of her daughter aloud with each wail. Other women relatives sitting with the mothers try to comfort them, but many among them also start sobbing. Shridevi wipes her tears with her sari and says, 'You know, I nurtured my daughter for years and brought her up with so many difficulties. And that morning, I saw her swinging from that mango tree in Chaudhary's garden. You know, I sat down under the mango tree looking at my own daughter's swinging body. I sat there for 14 hours. I kept on looking at her all the time. I remember her feet. The bodies started smelling under the sun. In those 14 hours, all I wanted was to bring her down close to my chest. But they said that we should not bring the bodies down if we want justice for our daughters. And so I kept on looking at her feet. When the police brought her body down after 14 hours, I ran to hold her in my arms, but they took me aside, wrapped her in a cloth and took her away immediately. I couldn't hold her for the last time. I still see her feet. Her body keeps on swinging in front of my eyes all the time.'

It's late evening and slanting orange rays of the setting sun are falling on Sohanlal's long face. His brother Jeevanlal is silent and still staring at the roof above his head. Sohanlal is now awake. His striped cream shirt and grey trousers are crushed. He opens his orange polythene bag and talks about how hopeful he is after the CBI took over the case from the Uttar Pradesh police. Then suddenly he stops and asks, 'Are you from the CBI?' I take a few minutes to get over my surprise. I re-introduce myself. I ask him what made him think that I may be from the CBI. He falls silent and looks at the people staring around him. His sense of paranoia is palpable. I try to reassure him.

After half an hour, Sohanlal slowly starts talking again. He starts the conversation by talking about the new fear in their lives. 'The Yadavs have raped and killed my daughters and now they are trying to frame us. The Yadavs are also going around the village saying things like "CBI comes in any form and they put the parents also in jail" and "Nobody can do anything to Yadavs under the Samajwadi Party government." They are trying to break us by making us scared. And now so many NGO people keep coming in and instructing us on what to say and how to say it to the CBI. I believe that the CBI will help us. Only they will ensure that my daughters get justice. But I am scared of the Yadavs. And the state government is of the Yadavs so it is always with them only. I am scared because the state government does not consider us as their *praja* (citizens). Because we are lower-caste Mauryas.'

Ram Babu joins us. Jeevanlal who has looked lost all afternoon also follows. But he still does not speak. Ram Babu says needlessly, as if he owes me an explanation, that the death of his only child has taken its toll on Jeevan. 'And they had to speak so much after their deaths. Hordes of media crew, politicians and activists kept coming in every day. He repeated the story of the death of his daughters a number of times. And then suddenly, he fell silent. Now he keeps on staring at people and walls around him.'

When I ask the brothers about the response of the Uttar Pradesh police from the first hours of the crime, Sohanlal starts recalling the sequence of events of that night.

## The night the children died

The evening of 27 May was a regular summer evening in Katra Sadatganj. With the fall of dusk, men came back from work. Kavita had helped cook dinner. The younger children of the village were eating dinner when Kavita and Ragini went to the fields to relieve themselves.

Sohanlal says, 'They went out to nearby fields to relieve

themselves. Since it was routine, nobody in the family bothered. At first, we thought that they must be standing in the village and talking to other women. We were beginning to get worried when Babu Ram came.'

Sohanlal's cousin Babu Ram is the sole eyewitness to the crime. When I met him, the 25-year-old farmer gave a full account of what he saw on the night of the crime. He said, 'I had gone to check the water in my fields between 8.30 pm and 9 pm on the night of 27 May. There, I heard the screams of the girls. When I flashed my torch, I saw Pappu Yadav dragging the girls along with four other men. I could not see the faces of the other four because the torchlight fell only on Pappu's face. I ran to intervene to protect the girls but Pappu put a *tamancha* (country-made revolver) to my head. I was terrified and ran away to inform my cousins about the abduction of their daughters.'

Sohanlal says that as soon as Babu Ram informed them about the abduction of their missing daughters, the family started their search. Propriety governed this search too. Sohanlal says, 'It was the matter of our girls, so initially we hesitated to spread the word and looked for them ourselves. But when we could not find them by 11 pm, we called all our relatives and all of us started looking for the girls.'

Then around 11.30 pm the brothers went to the Katra Sadatganj police chowki with 15–20 men from their extended family and community. 'But all the policemen were sleeping. It was very difficult to wake them up. After some time we managed to wake up Darogaji (outpost in-charge) Ramvilas Yadav. But the other four constables were not ready to get up. They first asked us our caste. When we told them that we are Mauryas, they slapped one of us. They verbally abused us and asked how "we" could dare to come to the police station to file a complaint. They said that our girls had run away and they'd come back themselves in two hours. They refused to help us.'

Sohanlal says, 'If our daughters had returned alive, we would never have gone to the police. But that night, we couldn't find them.' So the Maurya men refused to budge. 'But after some time, the Darogaji listened to us. We told him that our daughters had gone missing and pleaded for help. He listened and then looked for his uniform and put it on. But the four *sipahis* (constables) still didn't move. They took a lot of time to look for and then put on their uniforms. The Darogaji instructed Sipahi Chatrapal Singh and Sarvesh Yadav to come out and look into the matter, but they were not listening to him. But we kept pleading and after some time the Darogaji came out with them and they decided to go to Pappu Yadav's house.

'Then we went with the police to Pappu Yadav's house around midnight. But we found him at a neighbour's house near his home. When the Darogaji caught hold of Pappu, Constable Sarvesh Yadav and Chatrapal Singh started pleading with him right there in front of all of us to leave Pappu. They swore that Pappu was innocent and that they could vouch for him.

'I begged the Darogaji to interrogate Pappu and told him that he had abducted my daughters. After that, the Darogaji brought Pappu to the police outpost. After two slaps, Pappu confessed in front of the whole police station and all our relatives that he had abducted our daughters. Everybody heard this.'

And here is the part that explains the irresponsible behaviour of the police which led to their suspensions and arrests later. After Pappu Yadav confessed, Sohanlal says, 'Constable Sarvesh Yadav took Pappu aside and told him that if he went to jail as a rapist and thug, everybody'd make fun of him. If he went to jail after committing murder, then he'd earn a lot of respect in every jail.'

'In front of everyone?' I ask. Sohanlal confirms, 'Constable Sarvesh Yadav openly encouraged Pappu Yadav to kill my daughters in front of everyone at the police outpost. At least 20 people saw him saying this to Pappu.'

According to Sohanlal, after this Constable Sarvesh Yadav encouraged Pappu to say that the girls were with the eyewitness Babu Ram as the Darogaji looked on, standing quietly.

Sohanlal continues, 'It was clear now that the police were going to protect Pappu Yadav and help him harass us. So we decided to hire a jeep and travel to Badaun to meet higher officials.'

By the time the panicked families got organized, it was already 5 am. Sohanlal says, 'Constable Sarvesh Yadav saw us heading to Badaun headquarters in the jeep. He shouted out that our girls may be hanging on a mango tree somewhere in the village.' Unfortunately, the men thought it was more of the same inhumanity he had displayed all night. 'We kept going. But we'd gone barely 4 km away from the village when we got the news that our girls had actually been found hanging on a mango tree in the village. We ran towards Ramnath Chaudhary's orchard. I saw their swinging bodies and I fainted.'

It isn't clear yet how the girls were killed or exactly who killed them. That morning as the angry Maurya families gathered around the mango tree protesting against the police, the police tried to bring the bodies down. The girls' uncle Jai Singh says, 'The police kept on pressing us to bring the bodies down. But they had not arrested Pappu Yadav nor had they registered our complaint. On the contrary, a huge police force

and water tankers were deployed in front of Pappu Yadav's
house so that no one could harm him or his family. So we
didn't let them cut the bodies down. The police started acting
after the media came in. A local photographer clicked pictures
of the hanging girls that brought in immediate national media
attention to the case. Then the police noted the first entry
in their station diary (not the FIR) on 28 May at 4.30 pm.
We had already been sitting under the dead bodies of our
daughters for nearly 12 hours by then.'

The terrifying images of the two girls hanging from the
mango tree sent shock waves across the world with its echoes
of the lynchings of blacks in the American South. Everyone
from Congress scion Rahul Gandhi to Bahujan Samaj Party
(BSP) supremo and former chief minister, Mayawati, paid
quick visits to Sohanlal's home. Soon after, Lok Janshakti Party
leader Ram Vilas Paswan also spent time in Katra Sadatganj
with his son Chirag Paswan. Around a week later, when the
matter started taking a political turn, Chief Minister Akhilesh
Yadav began taking action, with pique and irritation that he
did not try to hide.

The entire five-member staff of the Katra Sadatganj police
outpost was suspended two days after the death of the girls.
An FIR was registered against Pappu Yadav and his brothers,
Avadesh Yadav and Urvesh Yadav. All three were arrested for
gang-raping and murdering two minor girls along with two
other unidentified accused.

The three brothers and policemen Sarvesh Yadav and
Chatrapal Singh were arrested and the case was moved to a
fast-track court. Soon after their arrest, during interrogation,
two of the accused reportedly confessed to the crime in front
of the UP police. Facing global criticism for the pathetic
situation of law and order in Uttar Pradesh and the blunders

of the UP police in the Badaun double murder case, the
state's chief minister soon agreed to a CBI investigation into
the matter.

As Sohanlal waits for the CBI to crack the case and identify
the murderers of his daughter and niece, he goes over his
painful memories of dealing with the police. 'My daughters
could have been saved if the police had taken my complaint
seriously and acted on time. But they kept on wasting the most
crucial hours that night in trivial arguments and as a result, I
found the hanged bodies of my daughters, swinging in the air.
They wanted to blame us for the killings. Had the media not
shown the truth to the world, they would have easily framed
us right then,' he adds.

The family alleges that the biased attitude of the police
continued even when the Special Investigation Team (SIT)
began their investigation on 6 June. Babu Ram, the witness,
says, 'Their caste bias continued in all further levels of
investigations. First at Kotwali (the police station at Usait)
they tried to change our testimonies themselves in the written
records. One of our boys who knew how to read found that
the answers written by the police were very different from what
we were saying. The UP police was intentionally changing our
answers to implicate us and protect the accused. Then they
started throwing weird questions at us, intended to confuse
and break us. We could feel in their conversations that they
wanted to save the accused because they are Yadavs. They
were also angry with us for "creating a hue and cry" in front
of the media. We are very scared of the Uttar Pradesh police.
So later, we collectively decided that we would not talk to the
SIT team when they took over the case on 6 June. And we did
not speak to them. We are poor illiterate people and they are
adamant about framing us. So we decided that we will only
speak to the CBI.'

Back to Badaun. Retired Inspector-General of Police (Uttar Pradesh) S.R. Darapuri says that he feels disgusted by the shameful show put up by the UP police in the Badaun double murder case. Over the phone he tells me, 'The response of the Uttar Pradesh police to the Badaun rape and double murder case has been highly irresponsible and evasive. The killing probably happened after the parents approached the local police outpost for help. But the outpost staff did not act on time and all major crucial evidence was lost due to their lethargy and criminal carelessness. Instead, they ridiculed the family and harassed them with casteist remarks.' He goes on to add, 'Evading filing FIRs is a regular pattern in the Uttar Pradesh police. And yes, there is a very strong casteist sentiment in the UP police.'

Another veteran Uttar Pradesh former top cop known for his massive police reforms' initiative is the former Director-General of Police Prakash Singh. About the UP police's response to the Badaun incident, he says, 'UP cops have a conducive role in the horrible Badaun crime. Local police outpost officers worked hand-in-glove with the accused and connived with them to execute the brutal hangings. And the UP DGP's statements on the matter are particularly disappointing. Clearly, floating honour killing theories and denying the rape of one girl are attempts to confuse the case and divert attention of people.'

～

As I come close to the end of my reporting trip, there is talk of putting the parents of the dead children through polygraph tests. It remains to be seen whether they will escape the elaborate Chakravyuh a vengeful state can set up if it wishes to. My last conversation in Katra was after sunset outside

Sohanlal's house, where the village residents were sitting quietly. Absentmindedly holding green mangoes in their hands, they talked about the dead girls. I was hoping to not have to hear the innuendo and slander that usually accompany cases like these. But 35-year-old Moolchand Shakya and 60-year-old Durgpal Shakya only said: 'They were both very nice children.'

## Second reporting trip—April 2015

I again went to Badaun in April 2015. At this point of time, the CBI had already filed its closure report and had concluded that the girls have committed suicide because of the shame of the affair of the older cousin being discovered. According to the closure report and all other forensic reports accessed by this reporter, the agency noted that there was no forensic or circumstantial evidence suggesting rape and murder as alleged in the FIR registered by the Uttar Pradesh police.

The CBI investigations, multiple examinations of forensic evidence, DNA profiling reports, multiple 'scene of crime' recreations and the results of a multi-institutional medical board constituted to look at the case—all indicated towards one direction. That Kavita was having an affair with the prime accused Pappu. The two girls had gone to meet him on their own on the fateful night of the crime. After being discovered by a family member, the girls got frightened about their honour and the consequences that would follow and so—according to the CBI—kept hiding till 2'o clock in the night. Then they walked to the mango tree, climbed up themselves, tied knots in their dupattas and hanged themselves to death.

The families of the victims have dismissed the CBI theory as devastatingly unbelievable and rubbish. The fathers feel that the CBI has got no answers to who killed their daughters. So they are de-railing the case by putting in baseless theories. Also important to mention is the fact that at this point in time all accused are out on bail. The CBI did not file charges against the accused citing 'lack of evidence'. The family has challenged the CBI's closure report in court and the CBI has filed objections to their 'protest appeal' submitted in Badaun's special court. Now, back to my second trip to Katra Sadatganj.

The trip was originally planned for reporting some other story but on my way back I felt a strong urge to know the current situation in Katra Sadatganj. The reporter in me was overpowered and I drove 140 kilometres off my scheduled track to make this unplanned unannounced visit to Katra Sadatganj.

The second half of the day had set in as I reached the mango tree by 3.30 that afternoon. The media camps earlier extended under the mango tree had all vanished now. The village was wrapped in a gloomy lull. Lying on the cots in the mud porches of their huts, old men were enjoying their post noon siesta while children were playing with glass marbles on the streets. I couldn't spot heavy deployment of CRPF force this time as I came closer to the victims' residence.

Moving away from the main village road, I crossed a dark muddy lane to reach Sohanlal and Jeevanlal's two-room hutment. Women of the house were sitting in the covered courtyard. I remember seeing auspicious Hindu symbols being painted all along the courtyard walls. An infant lying on a cot was constantly crying. Other children were playing around.

Sohanlal was drawing water from the only hand-pump in his house. He looked exhausted and weak. In a couple of seconds he recognized me and asked me to sit on the cot. Meanwhile he took a quick bath, wrapped a checkered lungi around his waist and settled on the mud floor of his courtyard.

Sohanlal's eyes became moist as he started the conversation with folded hands. *'Bahut dukh diya CBI walon ne madame, bhagwan kisi ka saamna CBI se na karwaaye* (CBI gave us a very hard time madame, I wish to god that no one has to ever face the CBI),' he started.

I felt that Sohanlal was much more fearless but more vulnerable than before. The CBI investigation that he was banking all his hopes on had, according to him, failed him and his daughters.

'It was overwhelming for us. I had demanded a CBI investigation into my daughters' rape and murder because I believed that only the premier investigative agency of the country could ensure us justice. But I now feel like the CBI team had made up their mind even before starting the investigation. Throughout the investigation they kept on trying to shift the blame on us.'

Sohanlal added, 'They started asking me weird questions. For example: "Have you ever been to the zoo? Have you ever travelled to Rajasthan? Have you ever gone to Calcutta?" I would say, "No, sir." Then they would ask: "When Pappu was killing you daughter, did you see? Were you present when Pappu was hanging your daughter to the mango tree?"'

At this point, Sohanlal's voice became thicker, and quietly, he started sobbing. 'I would say which father on earth would stand and see his child being killed and hanged? How could I be present there? What kind of questions were these? The CBI started questioning us early morning and kept on asking question like these till 11 in the night. While other people were being investigated in this case—for example a UP police cop—they were let off after 20 minutes of questioning. When I questioned and asked the CBI team why we were being tortured like this, they said, "*Tu zyaada tez ban raha hai, tujhe fansayenge* (You are acting too smart, we will ensure that you are booked in this case)." I put my head on their feet and said, I want only justice for my daughters, sahib. You do whatever you wish to do but please see that my children get justice.'

The father further complains that the CBI field officers deployed to work on his case were all residents from villages situated near Katara. 'Field Officer Arvind Singh who is investigating our case has his relatives spread all around this area. He and all higher officials of the agency come to our home and tell us to not say a word against the main accused Pappu. They tell me to transfer all my family's children to other cities and to stop speaking against the main accused. Otherwise the main accused might kill and destroy our family. I said, "Sir, you are from the CBI. If you are suggesting I leave my village and keep quite against the accused, what can I say? You can do whatever you want, you are from the CBI. But nevertheless, I will fight this battle as long as I can."'

The family further complained that the CBI team misbehaved with them, threatened them, roughed up an 11-year-old kid of the household and worked only to prove that either the parents killed the girls or they killed themselves.

'I am going to ask this in court—the clothes that the CBI has sent for forensic examination are not of my daughters. If you test fresh or other clothes, how will you get any proof of the crime? We are poor people but we know the clothes of our daughters. We remember their clothes.'

In between, the women of the family and the mothers of the deceased girls started speaking angrily. 'The CBI is not bigger than god. *Bhagwan ke ghar me der hai, andher nahi.* (In god's house justice might be delayed, but it's never denied),' says Shridevi.

The family were terrified and paralyzed by the fear of the unknown. Sohanlal further said, 'I never imagined that the biggest investigative agency of India can victimize the victims like this. They defame my daughters. My children were happy cheerful individuals. They never even killed an animal. How can you believe that such small girls will climb up a tree and hang themselves? They would have come to us if there was any problem. My children would never kill themselves.'

Sohanlal and others in the family expressed a lot of shock in the way of CBI's functioning. "They will come to the village, drink milk, eat lunch and then go back to their rooms in town. Sometimes we used to feel that they only come here to eat. I explained the sequence of events to them so many times. Showed them all the places, answered every question they asked... but they never believed me. They don't know who killed our daughters so they want to put the blame on anyone. And we are illiterate poor labourers from a village. Easiest to blame in all cases,' said Sohanlal.

As I prepare to leave Katra Sadatganj, Sohanlal tells me that the family had to struggle and approach the court to get their copies of all case-related papers. Even the police protection given to his family was removed for a couple of months until recently.

'I told this to judge sahib in court and he asked me to meet the SP. The accused are all released on bail. Their house has protection but the force was pulled out from my house. You tell me. The CBI did not allow the media to come in. They took away police protection. I live here with women and children. Who will be responsible if something happens to us? The SP ordered and gave us two guards just three days ago.

The SHO is angry with us now. He asked how we dared to
inform court about the removed force and approach the SP?
I folded my hands and begged for the security of my family
but he kept on hurling abuses,' he said.

~

In December 2015, the POCSO court of Badaun rejected
CBI's closure report. In a written verdict of 25 pages,
additional district judge Virendra Kumar Pandey dismissed the
CBI's closure report and summoned the prime accused Pappu.

Though both Sohanlal and Jeevanlal know that they are
in for a long long legal battle here, but still the dismissal of
CBI's closure report brought some respite and validation for
them. Sohanlal, who never sat on a train before has now
learned to travel frequently between Badaun and Allahabad
where he has to often go for case-related paper work for his
daughters.

The children's parents still believe that their daughters were
raped, killed and brutally hanged from the mango tree. They
tell me that they are going to fight this battle till the end—for
the sake of the grace of the memories of their daughters.

As I end this chapter, I think of CBI's closure report and
the feet of the hanging girls. In its closure report, CBI went to
the extent of saying that the younger sister was also desirous
of a relationship with the same man—the prime accused in
the case. In its report, CBI bases its observation on an alleged
phone conversation that happened between the younger girl
and the accused on the morning of 27 May 2014. I have read
the details of the conversation, and I feel that the conversation
has nothing which can suggest that the younger victim was
'desirous of a relationship' with the prime accused. Rather,
CBI's observations in this case suggest that the patriarchal

mindset of the team has overpowered their scientific approach in this particular matter.

~

The assumption that honour is greater than life for the women of this country was shaped by men. Human dignity is as important for women as for men. As far as life is concerned, who wants to die? More to the point, who wants to die for something as nebulous as 'honour'? If allowed an informed choice, I feel all women—just like all men—will choose life over death and the loss of one's so-called 'honour'.

# 9

# Sexual Abuse and Rape of Children

## 'What are we doing to our children?'

I AM STANDING AT THE PUBLIC SQUARE OF A DELHI SLUM situated on the outskirts of one of the metropolis' south-western suburbs. It's September of 2013 and the sun is unusually bright this afternoon. I am waiting for someone to pick me up from here—the landmark temple located right at the centre of this public square. Ten more minutes to go. I stand waiting and, meanwhile, look around.

In a long shot frame, I can see the sky piercing the tops of Delhi's skyscrapers, dotting the horizon till my line of vision ends. Whereas, just 10 feet ahead of me I can see around 15 women standing, sweating and fighting, to fill water in their pots from the only functional public tap available in this part of the urban slum. It took me a change of three modes of public transport and 100 minutes to reach here from central Delhi.

It's around 12 noon and I am on the second day of my period. The sun is burning my skin and heating my scalp. I feel dizzy for a moment. But then I drag myself back to my senses as the fight for water among the women intensifies. I see a couple of young men lurking around and laughing at the fighting women. Also, foul smelling water is oozing out of an open sewer nearby. Old polythene wrappers and dirt are all around. Children are eating cheap snacks from a small roadside shop on the pavement. Houseflies are buzzing around this makeshift shop and the eatables on display.

I am feeling a bit nauseous by now. I take out my water bottle from my bag. My water bottle—filled with purified and cold water—instantly reminds me of my privilege.

Ten minutes have passed and the water-fight near the public tap has slowed down. The first batch of women has filled their colourful plastic pots and is carrying them back home. Just then I get the phone call I was waiting for.

A couple of more phone conversations and we find each other. I see a timid looking, thin and short man walking towards me with speed. He was wearing an off-white shirt with dark brown loose trousers. Side parted and neatly combed hair. A shadow of deep melancholy ran through his long oval face. He looked weak. His sunken cheeks and drooping eyes remind me of Raskolnikov.

We shook hands and started walking almost immediately. Increasing my pace to match his, I almost ran behind him. We passed through a maze of narrow allies and non-existent muddy pathways to reach a multi-storey building located deep inside the slum. Populated entirely by migrant labourers, the building had at least 15 one-room houses on each floor with a couple of common toilets lined up at the end of each corridor. The air felt thick, smelly and seedy. I crossed a dark tunnel-like corridor on the second floor and stopped at the door of a corner house.

As the man opens the door, I see five-year-old Gudiya for the first time. She is wearing a printed cotton frock and has two pretty ponytails on both sides of her head. Her three-year-old brother is playing with her. Carrying a black slate and white chalk in her hands, she runs towards the man screaming, 'Papa, Papa! Look what I have drawn!'

Gudiya's father lifts the child up in his arms, pats her back and kisses her forehead. By now, her mother has also walked in from the small cooking area—a makeshift kitchen—in the one-room house. She is standing next to us holding her second child, her son, in her arms. As I greet her with folded hands, she breaks into tears.

She is a mother who has been through her five-year-old daughter being brutally gang-raped and then swinging between life and death for weeks.

I look at the mother's eyes. They are full of tears, swollen and reddish. I feel blank but I quietly give her a gentle one-shoulder hug and request her husband to bring some water for her. She takes one or two sips of water and keeps the glass away. After a few minutes, she looks slightly better. But nothing that I had witnessed in my journey this morning—or since the morning I was born—could have ever prepared me for this conversation. But before coming to the conversation, an important recap is necessary.

~

The nationwide uproar at the 16 December 2012 gang-rape in Delhi had not yet simmered down. But in mid-April 2013, the news of two men raping a five-year-old-child for two days in eastern Delhi broke. As details started coming in, it was revealed in medical examination reports of the child that candles and plastic bottles were inserted in her private parts. She went missing on 15 April and was rescued two days later on 17 April. Her body was covered in blood and dirt when she was discovered from a locked basement room of the building where she lived with her parents at that time.

As the girl was rushed for treatment in one of Delhi's premier hospitals, Delhi came to a boil again. Angry protestors came onto the streets. Candlelight vigils and prayers for 'Gudiya', the nickname given to the child by the Indian press, started pouring in from all quarters. She was on the brink of death but started responding to her treatment quickly.

Four days after the incident, Delhi police caught 22-year-old Manoj Kumar Sah and 19-year-old Pradeep Ram from Bihar. The main accused in this case, both men were migrant labourers from Bihar. They used to work as electricians and were living in the same building inhabited by Gudiya's family.

Since April 2013, Gudiya spent four months in hospital and underwent six major surgeries during this period including a colostomy. It took her a long time to be able to urinate properly again. She has still not recovered completely.

～

September 2013 is coming to an end now. Gudiya is drinking milk and playing in her house. Her mother wipes the milk moustache off her face with her sari's pallu. 'When my daughter went missing on 15 April, we registered a complaint with the local police immediately. But the police didn't listen to us. They denied registering our complaint and asked us to look for her ourselves. It was only after the media started showing everything on TV that the police got into action and went hundreds of kilometres till Bihar to catch the accused. If only they had gone to our building—a stone's throw away from the local police post that day! If only they had come in and searched the building—just the building—only the building... my daughter could have escaped the two days and nights of brutality that she went through. Everything was in the hands of the cops but they treated us like shit because we are poor people. They shooed us away, asked us for money and paid no heed to prayers and requests. By god's grace, the child survived. But are the police not also responsible for her condition along with the accused?'

The mother goes on and on. She is raging with anger and rightly so.

The father has been listening to his wife and nodding with a face that exudes both burning rage and vulnerability at the same time. Then slowly he starts talking. 'The doctors told me that she is doing fine now. She can go to school. Now my only concern is getting my children admitted to school. When the case was highlighted by the media, everybody was talking about what happened to us. What can I say; Sonia Gandhi herself came to visit my child. She assured us that the girl's health and education will be taken care of. Then another political leader from Gandhinagar—the eastern Delhi suburb where we used to live—a local leader called Arvinder Singh also came and promised that arrangements will be made for both our children's education. But we have not received anything from the government or anyone except for the expenses incurred during Gudiya's treatment and surgeries.'

Five months since the incident, the family is fighting on multiple fronts. Gudiya's father continues, 'Sonia Gandhi met our daughter and left. She assured her in front of the media but nothing happened. Then we went to Sheila Dikshit with folded hands. She turned us away saying, "I get 500 rape complaints every day. How many will I look into?" She told us to handle the matter on our own. During this whole journey, only the media and some members of the Aam Aadmi Party supported us. For the past five months, *India Today* is paying the rent of our room. A lady reporter has even agreed to teach our child. But I'm surprised why the government is not helping us!'

The hapless situation becomes more ironic with the children clinging to their parents and asking, '*Papa ham school kab jayenge?* (Father, when will we go to school?)'

As I prepare to leave, Gudiya's father informs me that he has to take the same metro train as me. We decide to walk together till the metro station. I kiss the child goodbye, hug the mother and leave the house with the father walking ahead.

~

After crossing through the maze of narrow allies and cramped houses, we reach the main road outside the periphery of this urban slum. Gudiya's father looked a bit relieved after stepping out of the claustrophobic environment of his living space to the wide open roads of the capital—lined with municipality-grown trees on either side. We now started walking side by side and he started talking.

'We have changed four houses in the past five months. I cannot tell you in words how painful all this has been.'

I nod quietly and listen as he goes on.

'I came to this city to make a life for myself and my family. I wanted us to get rid of the poverty of our village life. My wife and children used to live in the village earlier. They came only a few weeks before all this happened. My wife knew nothing about urban life. We come from Mithila in Bihar. Have you heard of Sitamarhi district ever? I come from there. Every year floods come and destroy our lives in the village. So I thought of coming to the city. A couple of months after I started working as a labourer here, I fetched my wife from Bihar to this city. The children also came. I was happy when they came because I used to feel very lonely in the city. Initially she felt scared in the city. One day she said that she feels as if the city is just like the river in Mithila. It will engulf us all. I didn't understand then but I do know now what she meant.'

I see tears hanging at the brim of his eyes. We both stop at a footpath for a moment as he continues. 'We used to live in Gandhinagar. The area was the same as where we live now. We had to leave that house after all this happened to my daughter—because the neighbours used to talk badly about us and my daughter. They would say things that hurt. The accused lured my daughter into their basement room by offering chocolates and chips. She is a child. She trusted them so she went in. But some neighbours would say that we didn't take good care of our children and that my daughter was greedy. It was so painful that we left that area. We had to change again and again—because whenever people would get to know about our daughter, things would become difficult. Now finally in this area, we are anonymous. Nobody knows us and our history. We cannot go back to our village in Bihar because the media reached there and everybody knows about the case. So it's better here.'

We have now reached the metro station. I have my metro pass with me. Gudiya's father buys a ticket for central Delhi and we board the same train. In a crowded coach, we stand facing each other, holding the handles hanging from the top to support ourselves.

I have no answers to give to the child's father so I keep quiet and listen.

He looks around, keeps quiet for a couple of minutes. I could sense that the anonymity of this swelling urban metropolis gives him a kind of refuge. The anonymous crowd around him made him more comfortable than the known faces of his residential mohalla.

After two stations, I tell him that he must carry on his legal fight and that he must educate his children. He asks me if I know a good lawyer. I give him a few contacts of the best human rights lawyers of Delhi I know of. But in my heart I have little hope about any of them taking up his case.

We are now reaching the end of our journey. He tells me that he does not work as a labourer anymore... he has started selling vegetables on a wooden cart.

'After what happened to my daughter, I think it's most important for me to educate her. If she doesn't study, who will support her later in life? She must learn to be self-sufficient and to stand on her own feet. You know how our society treats rape victims, don't you?' he says.

I look at him and nod quietly.

As we get out of the train coach and start walking towards the exit of central Delhi's most crowded metro station, I shake his hand for the last time and bid him goodbye.

I keep looking at the frail silhouette of his body till he disappears in the anonymous crowd that makes him feel comfortable.

~

Sexual crimes against children have been rising at an unprecedented rate in India.

The National Crime Records Bureau's (NCRB) data speaks volumes about how India is becoming an unsafe place for children.

10,854 cases of rape were registered under Section 376 of the IPC and under Sections 4 and 6 of the POCSO Act in 2015. In 2016, this figure soared up to 19,765.

In 2016, maximum number of rape cases involving children was reported in Madhya Pradesh (2,467),

Maharashtra (2,292), Uttar Pradesh (2,115), Odisha (1,258) and Tamil Nadu (1,169).

With every passing day, the graph of sexual crimes against children has been growing in India. Even conversations around demands for capital punishments for rapists of minors and stringent laws like POCSO are unable to bring the crime graph down.

~

When it comes to children, girls are not the lone victims. In September 2012, I travelled 400 kilometres away from Delhi to reach the Kuthaund police station area in the Jalaun district of Uttar Pradesh.

Here, an eight-year-old school boy was molested and raped by a constable deployed at the local police outpost of the village.

From the district headquarters in Jalaun, I travel for 60 minutes on a patchy broken road to reach the victim's village. His family lives in a small hut situated at the periphery of the village—in the *harijan tola* (scheduled castes' hamlet).

As I enter the village, the first thing I am told by local reporters is that 'the boy was born into a very poor Dalit family but was exceptionally good in studies'. As I walked through the village toward the victim's house, I thought, how feudal and casteist our villages are. Spaces where people are still living in ghettos based on their castes; spaces where a brilliant Dalit student still surprises people. Or are Indian villages just a raw mirror of the casteist ugliness that the city people are able to hide cleverly?

Lost in thoughts, I reached the boy's house. It was a one-room hut made of mud and hay. There were a couple of utensils lying around. An old woman was sitting at the door of the hut.

The boys' parents were not at home. They had gone to the nearest town to work as labourers at a construction site. The mother lifts bricks, the father ferries bags of cement from big trucks to the construction site on his shoulders. The boy was in Class 2 and he was also not at home. It was his school time and he was off studying in the village's only primary school. The old woman is the boy's grandmother. I sit with her inside the hut. After a few minutes of awkwardness, she starts talking in a thick Bundelkhandi accent.

'Last month my grandson was playing with his cousin in the village. It was afternoon and we were all taking a nap. The children went to the village grocer's shop and started playing there. My grandson lifted a 10-rupee note lying at the counter of the shop. That was his only fault for which he was punished so badly,' the grandmother says and starts sobbing.

Wiping her tears with her sari, she said that the shop-owner got mad at the children for picking up the 10-rupee note. 'He caught hold of my grandson, dragged him to the nearest police outpost and handed him over to Constable Kripa Sindhu Bharti.'

Flouting all rules and regulations of the Juvenile Justice Act made for dealing with 'children in conflict with law', the constable kept the child captive inside the police station for two days. He made him wash the floors of the police outpost, clean and mop. Then he made the child do oil massages on his body.

The grandmother says she feels horrified to remember the events of the past 20 days. As locals start gathering around, she feels uncomfortable. I request everyone to leave and then sit closer to her.

'He did wrong things to my child. He forced himself in his mouth multiple times. We were all crying and looking for him everywhere for two days. We thought he was missing initially. Later we got to know that daroga sahib has kept him at the *thana*. When he returned home, both his cheeks were swollen. There were scratch marks all over his body. He was depressed and unusually quiet. He stopped eating. For one week my boy kept shivering in high fever. I pleaded many times... but he wouldn't eat... wouldn't tell us what happened,' she said.

Ten days after returning home, the eight-year-old boy confessed to his mother that he was sexually assaulted at the police outpost.

After reporting the story, I spoke to everyone from the district superintendent of police (SP) to the range's inspector general (IG) to know about the action taken against the accused constable. All I was told was that the constable has been transferred and line attached. 'We are investigating the matter. Charges will be filed against the concerned police constable after our internal enquiry is over,' said R.P. Chaturvedi, the then SP of Jalaun district.

Back in the village, the boy's old grandmother believes that their case was not heard properly because they are poor and Dalit. 'I am a poor old woman. Over that, I am a Dalit. What value do my children hold to this country and its politicians and its police *wallaahs?* You tell me, daughter, suppose if my boy was the son of some big police officer or some politician or some big rich urban fellow—could any of this have happened to him?'

The family of the victim has been facing pressure to withdraw its complaint since the matter came out.

The grandmother further tells me, 'The other day, that constable came to our house at midnight. He was drunk. He threatened that he will kill us if we do not withdraw the case. Now you tell me, what should we do. We are poor people.

Nobody dares to touch the children of the upper-castes and the rich. All this is happening to us because we are lower-caste and poor people. So our children are vegetables or animals. The grocer can get my eight-year-old thrown in for a 10 rupee note and the daroga did all wrong things with him and got away with it. Is there any justice for my child?'

~

As news items about the rape of children as young as three years old are becoming the new regular, we must realize that we are leaving behind a much crueler world for our kids than the world we inherited. There is no denying the fact that something must be done to change this situation and make the world a safer place for our children. But that 'something' cannot be and should not be limited to making laws more stringent and vouching for capital punishment. Then what is it that needs to be changed? The answer perhaps lies within ourselves—in the dignity of our humanity which we are losing everyday, bit by bit.

# 10

# Rape As a Tool for Establishing Caste Supremacy

IT WAS A NIPPY DECEMBER MORNING OF THE YEAR 2014. IT was a little past 8 am. And a thick blanket of quintessentially eastern Indian dense winter fog was spread across the skies of Dumariya village in the Bhojpur district of Bihar.

During October 2014, just a couple of months before my arrival in this village, six girls of the Musahar community were gang-raped by upper-caste men here. The Musahar community of Bihar belongs to a sub-caste of Dalits. Traditionally associated with rat-catching, it still forms the lowest section in the ladder of social development. Coming at the end of hundreds of sub-castes of Dalits, Musahars form one of the most marginalized communities of India.

One has to drive around 120 kilometres from Patna via Ara town to reach the Piro sub-division of Bhojpur. One then turns towards Tarari block of this sub-division to reach Dumariya village. I left Patna around 5 am that morning to ensure that I reach Dumariya village before the villagers leave for their daily jobs in fields and otherwise. Musahar tolas (Musahar hamlets) are normally situated outside the village borders in most regions of Bihar. After stopping at the end point of the village, I walked across 600 metres of open fields to reach the Musahar tola of Dumriya.

It's around 9 am now, on a windy and cold eastern India December morning. In this bone-chilling environment, I see some toddlers of the Musahar community playing with wet sand and singing folk songs in Bhojpuri. Some of these kids were scantly clothed while others were naked. Before entering the story of the six Dumariya girls, it's crucial to understand where they are placed in the social order of this village.

In this village of 1000 households, around 30 per cent families are upper-caste, 30 per cent other backward castes (OBC) and 40 per cent Dalits. Most of its 400 Dalit families live in two ghettos—the villagers call them 'chamar tolas'. On the other hand, the 30 Musahar families of the village are not allowed even in the 'chamar tolas'. They occupy a separate, muddy settlement beyond the main village.

The Musahar tola of Dumariya village is situated around a large neem tree. A few low mud huts and four semi-pakka houses (that were built in 1998 under the Indira Aawas Yojna) stand near this neem tree. A few hens and two small goats are running around some wet fodder lying on the ground. There were old stale clothes scattered here and there.

Far away from the glitter of urban India or even the ecosystem of urban metro slums for that matter—the Musahar hamlet is a completely different universe having its own sets of struggles and history.

Young Musahar boys of this village have gone out to seek work as daily wage labourers in cities like Kolkata and Vijaywada. Older men still work in the fields of upper-caste farmers in this village. Their working conditions still resemble the work cycles of bonded labour, though this practice is abolished on paper now. The women of the Musahar hamlet often collect and sell scrap to make ends meet.

After six girls from the community were gang-raped by three upper-caste men in October 2014, a government official visited the Musahar hamlet for the first time in 50 years. Following a media uproar on the gang-rape, the district collector of Bojpur came to the hamlet and promised pakka houses for everyone, a concrete approach road towards the Musahar hamlet, electricity and water. Among all these 'assurances', the only promise which was fulfilled was that of building a concrete approach road inside the Musahar hamlet of Dumariya village. It's important to mention here that Bihar had got its first Musahar chief minister in Jitan Ram Manjhi just a few months before the crime happened to the Musahar girls of this village.

But this was not the first crime that took place against Dalits in this village. The socio-political landscape of this region has a violent history of its own. Villagers inform me that two caste-based massacres, killing six backward caste people, happened here in the early 1990s. 'Three people of Kahar caste (a sub-caste of mahadalits in Bihar) were fishing when their hands and legs were tied down and stomachs were ripped apart by Ranvir Sena men. On the same day, within 24 hours, three people were killed in our neighbouring Dehri village also. This time the Ranvir Sena men had killed one Yadav, one Muslim and one man of Rajwar caste. It happened in 1994 when Laluji was chief minister,' says local villager named Sabruddin. Ranvir Sena was the infamous upper-caste militia which conducted caste-based mass murders of Dalits across south Bihar in the 1990s.

I am standing under the neem tree and the conversations around Dumariya's violent past have stopped now. During informal chats before interviews, I am told that the 30 families in Musahar hamlet have been living in Dumariya village for over 50 years now.

## A snapshot of the universe of the Musahar tola

The Musahars of this hamlet normally wake up around 6 in the morning and eat left-over food from the night before. Then they leave home in search of work. Men try to get daily wage work in the fields of upper-caste farmers or try to catch fish in nearby ponds. Women pick scraps like old shoes, slippers, used polythene bags, wood, old rusted pieces of iron or anything that they might manage to sell. They all come back early evening and eat a meal on good days. They sleep hungry on lean no-work days. No one in the Musahar hamlet has ever gone to school and no one can understand a written letter in any language.

A few minutes later, I introduce myself to the six survivors and sit with them on the newly built concrete approach road for a conversation under the December sun. The survivors speak in thickly accented Bhojpuri, the native language spoken in this part of the world. I speak decent Bhojpuri too—which helps us to break the ice between all seven of us sitting together in a circle on the concrete road of their hamlet.

During the time of this interview—that is in December 2014—five out of the six girls were still teenagers and four were minors with the youngest being only 11 years old. The eldest was 20. She was married with two children. Another girl was 18 years old and was married just few months before the crime happened in October. Her husband had left her after the news of the gang-rape broke in the area. The other four girls were unmarried. Unlettered, none of them has ever been to school. Before the crime changed their lives, they used to spend their days picking rags from Dumariya and nearby villages and ate whatever they could get to eat on their way.

They first curiously looked at each other. It took all seven of us a few minutes of silence before we could warm up to each other. Once they felt trust and comfort, they opened up their hearts for me. And I kept listening, with my ears as well as my soul.

The eldest of the survivors started the conversation by recounting the events of the day when the crime took place. 8 October 2014 was a usual morning in Dumariya village.

She said, 'Like every other day, on 8 October also, we all left home to collect scrap from nearby villages. All six of us were together. Our two younger brothers aged nine and 11 years were also with us. We collected scrap all day. I remember, that day there was a wedding in a nearby village. So we got a lot of waste scrap from there also. Then we went to nearby Kurmuri village to sell the scrap that we had collected during the day. Three men named Neelnidhi Singh, Jai Prakash Singh and Jaggu Ojha used to buy scrap in Kurmuri village. So we went to them and requested them to buy our scrap. They measured our scrap and took all our collected scrap from us. When we asked for money Neelnidhi Singh said that they don't have change. He told us that Jaggu pandit will go and get some change from nearby Fathepur. Meanwhile he ordered us to sit down and wait. While we were waiting, Neelnidhi and Jai Prakash were drinking alcohol. After some time, Jaggu pandit came with the change and he brought more alcohol with him. After this, all three of them started drinking. I requested them to give us our money as it was getting dark *(Malik hamaar paisa de da, aandhaar ho ta... ghar jay eke ba hamni ke)*. But he scolded us and said that we will have to stay back otherwise he will kill us with his gun. Then Jaggu pandit forced us to drink alcohol. Before we could understand what was happening, they tied our brothers with iron rods and started beating them! Then they grabbed us. One after another the three of them raped all of us. They were slapping us, abusing us, beating us and raping us. Our brothers were crying and pleading with them to leave us (*Didiya ke chod de, didiya ke chod de!*). They were screaming—leave my sisters, leave my sisters! But they threatened to kill our brothers and asked them to watch the crime and learn from it.'

By then the sun was up but all six of them sat frozen. Neelnidhi Singh, one of the rapists, was a former area commander of the Ranvir Sena. He was previously arrested in 2007, and charged in a 1994 murder case.

After a few seconds of silence the second eldest added, 'We begged, pleaded, folded hands and wept in front of them—screaming please let us go, please let us go. But they wouldn't let us go. They refused and threatened to shoot us. We know that *babu sahibs* (upper-caste men) have guns so we were scared. After a few minutes of being captive, we again started pleading. We said that we want go out to urinate. After a while, they allowed us to go for urinating but said that we should come right back after peeing. We said yes, quickly opened the ropes of our wounded brothers and we all ran away together as fast as we could. It was already dark. We were so scared that we did not look behind. We jumped across small rivulets that came in the way. We crossed the crop fields, running like wild animals and stopped running only after reaching home that night.'

By the time the girls reached home that night, it was 10 pm. No one in the hamlet had slept when they returned. Older men were sitting outside their huts waiting for the girls and the two younger brothers to return. Everyone was worried and feared some mishap in their hearts. Other habitants of the hamlet told me their intuition said that the children are dead. 'Thankfully, they returned alive that night. It was a big relief,' said an old man during one of the conversations. The residents of the Dalit ghettos of the village were outraged and wanted to file a police complaint.

The FIR was filed at the local Tarari police station on 9 October 2014. The three accused named in the FIR were: then 35-year-old Neelnidhi Singh, his 40-year-old brother Jaiprakash Singh and 55-year-old Jaggu Ojha. The case came into media limelight but the story quickly died out in mainstream media. Probably because of the geographical distance of the incident from 'Delhi'.

Jitan Ram Manjhi, the first Musahar chief minister of the state was receiving a lot of flak from the state media for 'increasing crimes against the Musahar community under his regime'. Responding to the criticism, the chief minister took up the case and issued instructions of quick investigations and a speedy trial in the matter. As a result, all three accused were arrested within 24 hours of the filing of the FIR due to direct pressure from the then chief minister.

The accused were charged for rape, atrocities against STSC act and POCSO Act. But despite medical reports of all six girls confirming strong possibility of rape, charges were filed only on the basis of the confirmed report of the youngest 11-year-old girl. All others were converted into witnesses.

Following the instructions of a speedy trial given by the then chief minister, additional district and sessions judge of Ara-Bhojpur, J.P. Mishra convicted all three accused of raping a minor Dalit (Musahar community) girl on 22 January 2015. Announcing the verdict on 28 January 2015, the judge awarded life imprisonment to all three accused. Twenty years of rigorous imprisonment under section 376 (D) of IPC and an added 10 years of imprisonment under the POCSO Act.

~

All six girls have been given a compensation of 90,000 rupees each from the state government. The girls told me that bank accounts in their names were opened in the Bihar Grameen Bank, and that they were given the first installment of 20,000 rupees each. But later, when they went again to the bank to receive their second installment, the bank manager turned them away, saying that the rest of the money will be used for some 'colony development work'. He said that the compensation money could be further dispensed to them only after they presented a written request before him from the block development officer to do so. The girls and everybody in the hamlet were surprised by the bank official's behaviour. Nobody had any clue of what to do about this.

Except the youngest 11-year-old one, all five girls have been given a compensatory job of cooking *khichadi* in the primary schools of three nearby villages. The girls don't like their work but they have no other choice. 'I don't like cooking khichadi. Because we have to cook in huge vessels—the vessels are larger than my size. All the time I feel nervous. I am always afraid that some day this hot steaming khichadi rice will fall on my body and I will die of burns,' says the eldest girl with her eye wide open.

In between our conversation about what happened to them, the girls talk at length about their fears of what might happen to them now. The second eldest tells me, 'We have been getting threats from the upper-caste people of Kurmuri village since the case went to the police. They are shocked that we "dared" to go to the police. They have warned us that they will cut us down, peel our skins off and then kill us (*kaat-cheel ke maar denge*). We are very scared. It is very easy for them to kill lower-caste people here. They have been killing us for years now. They can kill us any day. They rape us, beat us—they can do anything to us anytime they want. Out of fear, we have kept a bottle of poison with us. Because they are all merciless people. Don't you know, they slaughter Dalits very brutally here? I think it is better to die by drinking poison than by being slaughtered at the hands of these heartless babu sahibs.'

Later I spoke to Sudha Varghese, a social worker who is also locally known as '*cycle wali didi*'. Sudha Varghese has spent her life working among the Musahar community of Bihar. She was also awarded the Padma Shri in 2006 for her dedicated work towards the upliftment of this community which still hangs at the lowest level of the social ladder of progress in Bihar. Sudha had followed the case of the gang-rape of 6 Musahar girls in Bhojpur very closely. In a late February 2015 conversation she told me, 'I have met the victims several times, saw all important reports related to the case, met DSPs-SPs-Collectors and all other officers related to the case. And I know that a speedy trial has happened in this case. Investigation was quick and Bihar probably got its fastest conviction and a good verdict in a rape case delivered within a record six months time! But, despite all this good news I have been very disturbed by this case. Because even after strong medical reports of all six girls confirming rape, charges were filed only on the testimony of one girl! Even after Supreme Court has issued strict guidelines mentioning to file charges on the basis of testimonies of victims this is what is happening on the ground. All six girls were cross-examined and they again and again said that they were raped. But the chargesheet mentions only the youngest one as the victim and has turned all other girls as witnesses in the matter. I have spoken to all high rank officers related to the case and I strongly feel that things have been 'managed' to ensure that only one girl is shown as a victim. Later, as you might know, what is happening in all cases of mass massacres against Dalits in High Courts here in Bihar? Be it Bathani Tola massacre or Laxshmanpur Bathe massacre or now even the Shankar Bigha massacre. Take any of the above examples—lower courts convicted but all upper-caste accused were released from higher courts in these cases. The same might happen in this case too, I am afraid. A Dalit's life has no value here.'

After the lower court verdict came in, I spoke again to the Dumariya girls over the phone in February 2015. I felt that the girls were more scared after the verdict came out.

In a quivering voice, the eldest girl said, 'I know that they have been jailed but we are very scared. Their relatives have threatened us that they will kill at least 30 of us to avenge the conviction of their three men.' She fell silent for a few seconds. After that in a careful low pitched voice she added, 'A few weeks ago, one night we saw around 19–20 armed men standing around our tola and we thought they are going to kill us that night. But a security police camp has been set up near our tola now. I think that is why these armed men went away that night. But this does not take away the fear of being killed at their hands from our hearts. We have always lived in fear but since the verdict came out, we haven't been able to sleep at night. We constantly fear for our lives now. We know in our hearts that they can come and kill us any day because they are strong powerful upper-caste babu sahibs and we are lower-caste Dalit Musahars. They can do anything to us at anytime.'

The fact that even justice could not instill a sense of empowerment among the Bhojpur-Dumariya village survivors is a living testimony to the long way Indian society and the Constitution has to go before we reach a point of social security and equality.

~

Seoni is a small tribal district situated in the southern tip of Madhya Pradesh. Sandwiched between the other tribal belt districts of Mandla and Narsighpur, Seoni is a lush green district with a large forest cover. As I travel to Seoni from Jabalpur, I pass through a long stretch of dense forest zone on both sides of the road. This unending forest area reminded me of the celebrated history of the forests for Seoni—which were used as a backdrop by India-born British author Rudyard Kipling in his book *The Jungle Book*. But the next moment I remind myself that I have travelled 900 kilometres away from Delhi to Seoni to meet a family which is a living testimony of the numerous caste wars being fought in post-independent India and how women's bodies are used as battlegrounds to fight these caste wars; the family for whom the green forest cover of this region and the consistent drizzle only trigger deep melancholy.

It's September of 2013. After a long drive from Jabalpur through the largely patchy roads, I reach Nirmal village in the Seoni district of Madhya Pradesh. Madhuram*, a resident of the Dalit colony of the village, has been waiting impatiently for my arrival. As I reach his house, I find him sitting outside on a plastic chair in the verandah. He tells me that he has been pacing up and down, waiting for me since the past 30 minutes.

I am quickly taken across his five-room pucca house, straight towards the innermost room. Three women of the family were waiting for me inside this last room. Two of them are around 50 years old while the youngest is about 30.

Madhuram's family are not natives of Nirmal village. They arrived here around nine years ago. Madhuram had told me that their native village also falls in Seoni district and is less than an hour away from here.

Nine years before this interview, after around 150 men of the Yadav Gowli community had attacked their home. It was the night of 8 July 2004. The three women of the family sitting with me now were alone at home that night. The Yadav mob of 150 men barged into their house, broke the door open and dragged the three women out. In an attempt to take caste-based revenge, 16 of the Yadav men gang-raped these three Dalit women.

The Gowlis are a pastoral Yadav community, traditionally working as milkmen. There were 125 Gowli and 12 Dalit families living in Madhuram's native village at the time of the crime.

On the morning of 4 July 2004, news broke in Madhuram's native village that a Chandravanshi minor girl belonging to the Gowli community has gone missing since the previous night. In a few hours, the Gowlis discovered that Madhuram's nephew Nitesh was also missing.

The boy and the girl knew each other well. The family tells me that the Gowli girl also used to visit their house sometimes. Meanwhile, back in 2004, the news spread like wildfire in the village. A Dalit boy had eloped with a Gowli Yadav girl. The love story quickly turned into a caste based 'honour' battle in the village. The Gowlis decided to avenge their 'lost honour' by raping the Dalit women of Madhuram's family. After the 4 July 2004 attack, the situation continued to worsen. Madhuram told me that after the gang-rapes, there was a steady rise in caste-based discrimination in his native village which forced the family to seek rehabilitation in nearby Nirmal village.

As I settled down for the interview, the three survivors were sitting quietly in the furthermost corner of their house. They remain silent for a good 15 minutes in the beginning. They said that they don't want to talk about the incident and that they wish to forget it like a bad dream. I understood their situation and apologized for intruding in their privacy. I almost got up to leave. Before leaving I made one request, saying that if they consent to share their story with me, it might help in increasing common people's understanding and awareness of caste-based violence and how it affects women. I also mentioned that their sanity and peace of mind are more important to me than knowing their story. They looked into my eyes, looked at each other and agreed to the interview. The next moment we were all sitting together on the floor of the last room of the house.

The youngest one started by talking about the fond memories of her lost home in the family's native village. She said, 'Ours was not a usual Dalit family. Unlike most Dalits in the rest of India, we had our own field... it was a small piece of land but we had our own. Our field received water directly from the canal so it was well irrigated. We even had fresh-water wells in our house. The men and women in our family never worked for the Gowlis. My husband was a secretary in the village panchayat. We wanted our children to get computer training. I think the Gowlis were annoyed with all this. They never wanted us to have our own wells, our own field and work for ourselves. Dalits were supposed to be always living at their mercy. How could they bear to see us sending our children to school or one of us becoming a secretary in the panchayat?'

The elder survivor joined in and said, 'When the girl and

boy went missing, we assured the Gowlis that we will help in looking for them. That night too, all the men in our house had gone out to Nagpur in search of their girl and our boy. But the fact is that it was never about the girl. The Gowlis had always had a grudge against us and we clearly felt it.'

She goes on, 'This incident gave them the opportunity that they had been waiting for since many years. More than their girl eloping with our boy, it was a matter of showing the "right" place to a prospering and strong Dalit family living in a Gowli-dominated village.'

At one point during the conversation, the women quietly start sobbing. The youngest gazes at the wall in front of her. I feel a sudden churning in my stomach.

After a short spell of silence, the youngest one gathers herself and wipes her tears with the corner of her soiled sari. Still gazing into the eternity of the wall in front of her she slowly says, 'I had gotten married two months before the crime. On the night of 8 July, we were anxiously waiting for the men of our family to return home. We were scared. We had locked all doors of the house from inside and were sitting huddled up together. The Gowlis had warned us that if we didn't return their girl by 8 July, they'd ruin us. That is why we were more nervous. Tension had built up in the village right from the evening. But what happened to us next was beyond our imagination.'

While the older women were gagged and raped by five and two men respectively, the young bride was attacked by nine men.

The youngest goes on detailing the sequence of events of that night. She adds, 'It was around 11 at night when they began knocking fiercely at our door. Before we could understand what was happening and prepare for running away or any such thing, the door broke open and lots of Gowli men barged into our house together.' Looking at one of the elderly survivors she continued, 'She was the first one to be dragged out. Then me and then my mother-in-law. There were many of them and we were only three women. We were dragged down, out of our house, to the road in front of everyone. We cried, screamed and yelled, but nobody listened to us. Our clothes were torn, we were beaten and they abused us in vulgar language. Then they took both my elder and younger mothers-in-law to separate corners. And then they took me to the other end of the village and raped us repeatedly.'

Nine years on, the three women tell me that they still live with the wounds of the crime fresh in their hearts and souls. The elder survivor said, 'We are living somehow. Just dragging ourselves day after day. Years might have passed, but we haven't been able to forget how the entire village saw us being dragged out of our house to the streets in torn clothes. We cannot forget how those men imposed themselves on us and raped us. We haven't been able to forget that night. We are dead inside.'

The 12 accused chargesheeted in this case have all been sentenced to life imprisonment. The verdict did bring much needed closure but has not eased the ongoing sufferings of the survivors and their family.

Talking about the psychological and physical situation of the three women of his family, Madhuram complains about the indifferent attitude of the state and central governments. He says that he has a long list of unfulfilled promises that were made to him after the crime happened to his family. 'We were uprooted from our village and given a piece of land outside this Nirmal village. How can anybody live outside a village? We had to spend our own money to build a house here in the

Dalit colony. Our land, our canal, and our wells, everything is lost now. The land that we have been given by the government in place of our well-irrigated fields is all barren. Nine years on, we haven't yet received the compensation amount promised by the government. We asked for guns for our own safety, but all we got was a license. How can we buy guns? We are not left with any money. We are barely able to make ends meet now. All three women of our family—the survivors—were promised jobs. But only the youngest—my daughter-in-law—has got a job. That too of a peon in a nearby school,' he says looking at me with his blank moist eyes.

He goes on, 'Now I feel that those promises were made to us only because the case had made headlines back then. Our government and administration are insensitive towards rape victims. Especially when the woman is Dalit, they turn a deaf ear to the complaint and her family. There is no one out there to listen to us.'

While I am talking to Madhuram, the youngest survivor gets ready for work. Saying a last goodbye outside the house, she holds my hand softly and whispers in my ear, 'Everyone in the school knows why I got this job. In this part of the world, no man would take back his woman after something like this happens to her. But I am lucky, my husband accepted me. But this job? This job is a struggle in itself. I know that I have no other option but to earn for my family. But I want to tell you one thing. There is something about this job which hurts me deeply. Every single day when I go on my duty, I am reminded of the fact that I got this job because I was gang-raped.'

# 11

# Rape and Sexism Inside the Indian Police Force

It is a late February morning in 2014 and I am at the town police station of Latehar district, situated around 1100 kilometres away from the national capital. Deep in the heavily forested core Maoist zone of Jharkhand state, the dark, damp and dingy interiors of the police station wear an unusually quiet and deserted look. Passing the empty central desk, empty lock-ups and running water taps, I find my way to the chamber of police station in-charge, Virender Ram.

Virender Ram hefts a heavy bundle of papers on the desk and says, 'This is the case diary of her gang-rape case. She is a constable here and I know that you have travelled from Delhi to meet her, because you think she should get justice. We are all working towards the same goal. You know how detailed the case diary we have prepared is? Our investigation in this case is already being talked about in police trainings sessions. But *she* isn't interested. *She* is not talking to anyone. She is happy and normal. I feel she isn't that keen on getting justice for herself. Besides, she is on leave now.'

In the Latehar police station, I go through the case diary and other documents related to what is now known here as the

Neetu Kumar gang-rape case. With every passing conversation about Neetu, the subtle whispered campaign against her is more and more evident. The personnel of this station have been maligning their own colleague for many months now.

On 20 August 2013, Neetu, a 27-year-old constable in Latehar district, was travelling in an SUV with her parents, brother and two other relatives from Ranchi to their village in Garhwa district. Neetu had been appointed constable after her policeman husband was killed in December 2011 in a Maoist ambush of independent MP Inder Singh Namdhari's convoy. Two years after her husband's death, she was barely piecing together her life—the new job, her two children.

But, in August 2013, it was no ordinary trip the family was taking. In the car was the corpse of Neetu's sister, who had been murdered along with her husband. The family intended to perform the cremation in their village, but as the grieving family drove down National Highway 75, they were to encounter another tragedy. Their car was stopped by a group of men who robbed the family and raped Neetu. Three days after the crime, Latehar police arrested five men for dacoity and rape.

Virender Ram says, 'They were all drunk. They blocked the highway and robbed 10 other vehicles also. All of them robbed her family but only two were involved in rape. Her vaginal swabs were tested and the DNA proved that two of them were involved in the rape.'

On paper, it seems as if her colleagues have treated Neetu with consideration. After the gang-rape, Neetu and her family asked for security. The Jharkhand police then transferred her to the women's police station of Latehar district and gave her residential quarters on the police station campus. There, her colleagues told me that she was on leave and had gone to her village for a family ceremony.

It's been six months since the event. When I ask Ram, the man in charge of the station Neetu once worked in, about her work, he says, 'Women constables here do regular duty. They are generally asked to come if there is any arrest involving women or for controlling women participants in public protests. Neetu was herself a constable here and clearly knew a complaint should be filed whenever a crime happens. But she did not come to the police station after being robbed and raped. Instead she went back to her rented accommodation in Latehar with her family.'

Smirking, he expresses surprise that Neetu didn't come to the police station first to register an FIR. 'When we got the information of these highway robberies and went to the spot, we found a ladies' purse and a gold chain lying there. One of the constables found her passport photo in uniform from that purse and so we identified her. When the next morning she was asked about how her purse, ATM cards, gold chain and other material was found on the highway, only then she told us that her family was robbed and she was raped.' The smirk widens into a smile when he adds, 'There were no signs of protest or resistance. The accused told us during investigation that she was repeatedly asking them to do whatever they want to do but to spare her life.'

He warns me that travelling to Garhwa district to meet Neetu will be useless. Then, almost chuckling, he sums up his sentiments. 'You want to meet her and you came here because you feel that she is raped, something bad happened to her. We feel the same… but if you see her she looks absolutely normal and happy. There's no trace of sorrow or stress on her face. Don't write it like this, but I think her character is not good. You can go if you want but I'd say that meeting her won't be useful.'

Despite the department repeatedly boasting about how everything is being done to ensure that Neetu Kumar gets justice, remains safe and keeps working, the undercurrent of hostility surfaces easily.

Assistant Sub-Inspector (ASI) Rameshwar Singh was one of the first police officers to reach the scene of the crime in the wee hours of 21 August 2013. On being asked about the case, the middle-aged man breaks into a similar indifferent grin. After a few minutes of casual conversation, he opens up about his doubts. 'The incident happened around 1 am, and we met her around 10 that morning, only when we called her. She is in the police force. Why didn't she come to us first? How could she go and sleep at her home after being raped? We filed the case, got her medical (test) done and did everything. But she wasn't keen to get justice because she is like that. She did not even resist while she was being raped. Everybody around knows how many affairs she has had. I can count them for you.'

I try to unpack the implications of what Singh and his colleagues are saying. As investigators, they aren't denying that Neetu was raped. The allegations instead are two-fold.

One, Neetu's response during the rape was not what they think women should do when confronted with rape—flail, cry and resist—even at the cost of their lives. They certainly should not try to negotiate.

Two, Neetu's response after the rape didn't follow their rulebook either. Death, violence, gang-rape on the side of a road when her sister's body hadn't been cremated yet. Even under these circumstances, they would have preferred it if Neetu had trotted up to the station and filed an FIR.

Somehow these two allegations add up in the ASI's mind to being the behaviour of a promiscuous woman.

At the Latehar police station, this ugly contempt was not limited to Neetu Kumar. In a conversation outside the police station, the ASI tells me about his views of women working in the police force. He says, 'Like Neetu, most of these women constables come on compensation appointments. They don't work at all and get a salary equal to us. They are almost like showpieces. Madame, you please write this with my name— that these women don't work but get equal pay. We have to take them to the sites of protest because only women can intervene with women protestors. But we have to keep an eye and take care of these constables too whenever we take them on any assignment.'

He adds, 'On the contrary, I think that all women should be removed from the police force. They don't have any purpose at police stations. They only create unwanted stress and problems. Whenever there is a women constable present at the police station, there is stress among policemen. We are not able to work properly. They do nothing but only distract, pollute the environment and so generally many people at police stations end up having illicit relations with them.'

In the women's cell of the Latehar police station, situated in a small building 10 metres away from the main one, I met four women constables working under a male in-charge and an assistant in-charge. Since it was established in March 2011, the women's cell of the Latehar police station has never had a woman in-charge. Lal Bahadur Ram, the head of the cell, says, 'Women do the usual *pehredari* and are taken to public protests to handle female protesters. We cannot treat male and female officers as equals. We (men) have to keep an eye on our female staff. Whenever they are sent out on any assignment, they are always escorted by male colleagues. We do all this to protect them.'

The women's cell has always been short of female staff. Station personnel say that this is because of the smaller proportion of female staff in the police overall. As Ram put it, 'Very few women apply and even fewer get through the physical tests.'

Of the four women constables sitting quietly in the cell, two were appointed on 'compensation grounds'—appointed in lieu of their dead husbands. Nanika Koi, Leelawati Devi and Pramila Devi are natives of Latehar district and have only attended school up to Class 10. The fourth, Poonam Kumari, is from the neighbouring Garhwa district and has a bachelor's degree.

They are quiet in the beginning, silent even about why they joined the service. Nanika and Leelawati say that they took up the job to run their households after their husbands died. They'd have taken any job, but this is the only one they got. Nanika slowly murmurs, 'It never occurred to me that things like motivation count in one's life. I've never had the luxury to think about liking my job or about empowerment. I had children to feed. I had to work.'

Pramila Devi, their colleague, says she has three children. Her husband was doing nothing. She had to do something to feed her family and a job as a police constable just came along. She smiles as she says, 'Everybody in the thana knows my husband. He often comes here to pick me up and drop me, or even just like that. He is closer to my colleagues than I am.'

Poonam is the only woman in the Latehar police station who talks about liking her work. Her face shines as she says, 'I like to be in the police. I feel confident. I think I can do something for my country and earn my own money through this work. But we always go out with our seniors as the world is bad for women. No woman is safe, not even us. One of our colleagues was raped last year. So we try to be careful.'

Since the Sixth Central Pay Commission's recommendations were accepted, the take-home salary of these police constables falls between Rs 17,000 and Rs 18,000. Their basic pay is Rs 7,100, with a 100 per cent dearness allowance, adding another Rs 7100 to their payment. They also get a food allowance of Rs 1,000, plus Rs 300 as medical allowance and other rotating allowances.

I ask if they mind being photographed. They pose happily inside the building. When I ask if they're willing to be photographed outside the gate of the women's cell, near the signboard, they're very reluctant. From the gate, they are in the line of vision of all the male officers of the main station and this, they tell me later, is what makes them hesitate.

~

To meet Neetu Kumar, you have to cross a heavily forested Maoist stronghold past ruined and deserted roads to reach the Anda-Mahua forest range in Bhandaria block of Garhwa district. Neetu's village is on the Jharkhand–Chhattisgharh border near Jashpur. Amid the wedding celebrations of a relative and a huge crowd gathered around her mother's home, she was anxious and initially refused to meet me.

Dusk has fallen by the time I reach her village. Surrounded by hordes of relatives, Neetu sits quietly on a plastic chair under the white, floral tent pitched in front of a pond and the wide open lane beside which her mud hut lies. A goods carrier loaded with wedding gifts such as a red almirah and plastic chairs stands in front of her and children dance all around. Dressed in a pink georgette sari and green bangles, Neetu comes to a corner of the open tent and sits with her child in her lap. Her brother and mother sit close by. She begins the conversation by saying she is afraid to talk to anyone at all about her situation—the complex predicament of a woman who faced sexual violence and happened to be in the police. She says, 'Normal women can talk to the media, criticize the police and express themselves. But I cannot. If I said anything to anyone, my department would say that I am bad-mouthing the police to the media. And I have to work there. I have children to feed.'

Her younger brother says quietly, 'We didn't go to the police when this happened to her because like any other family, we didn't want the matter to come out. It would bring a bad name to her and to us. And that happened. Her life isn't normal now.'

Recalling the night she was attacked, Neetu says, 'I have already lost my husband in conflict. That day my sister was murdered. Our family has seen too much violence. So when they dragged me out of the vehicle, I went quietly. Those who ask me why I did not resist, would they have come to feed my children had the men slaughtered me? I wasn't in a position to resist. I have lost too much in life to resist. I wanted to live because I had children waiting back home.' She cries silently and then begins looking up at the sky to calm herself. After a while, she gathers herself and speaks in a quiet rage about the complete absence of training that she or her female colleagues receive. They do 'regular duty' as ASI Rameshwar Singh said, but without the regular training that any man in the police force gets, setting them up to fail.

While calming down the child crying in her lap, she says, 'The other day, DIG sahib said to me that he will dismiss me because despite being a cop, I could not protect myself.' She doesn't rage further about her superior officer blaming her for getting raped.

She continues, 'I told him that I didn't know how to

protect myself. I was never trained like that. We never held a
pistol in our hands. We are trained only in holding a *danda*
(wooden stick), and not even properly. Our training was never
a matter of concern since most of us are not considered capable
of doing any serious work. But how can we protect others or
even ourselves without any proper training?'

When asked about her idea of justice for herself and her
plans for the future, she looks up at the sky again. After a
long pause, she slowly adds, 'I don't want my rapists to be
hanged because I am afraid that my family will be attacked
in retaliation. I want them to be behind bars. And I want to
live a normal, quiet and free life now. I want to do my work
and raise my children quietly. And I think the one thing that
I crave now is normalcy. I want to be able to just live normally
again. But I know this is not possible.'

~

On the morning of 9 September 2012, Sandhya Dharma
More returned as usual to her room after serving on the night
shift. Sandhya was a constable at the Karmad police station
in Aurangabad district, Maharashtra. Her father had travelled
from their home in Dhule district to meet her the previous
night and stayed over at Sandhya's rented accommodation right
in front of the police station. She turned 22 that morning.

Back from work, Sandhya said goodbye to her father who
was to leave for Dhule at 8 am. After sending him off, she
wrote a two-page-long suicide note and hanged herself. In
the afternoon, one of her colleagues came into her room to
wish her a happy birthday, only to find her hanging from the
ceiling fan. At the Government Medical College and Hospital,
Sandhya was declared dead on arrival.

Sandhya was recruited as a constable and posted in the

rural police station of Karmad around a year before her death. In her suicide note, Sandhya explained how she was being sexually abused and mentally harassed by Sub-inspector Yunus Shaikh for some weeks. She also wrote that constable S.V. Bandale had helped Shaikh torture her. Both Shaikh and Bandale were posted in the same police station and were Sandhya's superiors at work.

Immediately after Sandhya's death, Shaikh and Bandale were suspended from their posts. An FIR was also filed against them for abetting her suicide and for sexually and mentally harassing her. The case is under trial right now and chargesheets have been filed against both. Aurangabad-based journalist Mohammad Akeef, who has covered this case for the local media, says, 'My sources inside the police department informed me that Sandhya did tell her seniors in the department that she was being harassed at the Karmad police station, but nothing happened until she committed suicide.'

The circumstances leading to Sandhya's death form just one of the many dark stories that have become a common and invisible part of being an Indian policewoman.

Over months of my reporting on women in the Indian police force, I interviewed a number of male and female police personnel cutting across the ranks from constable to inspector-general. As in the cases of Sandhya and Neetu Kumar, incidents of policewomen being sexually harassed or bullied at work are extremely commonplace. Sometimes these stories make it to the papers. Mostly they don't. There are a few success stories among the women in the police force. But even those women who are lauded as unequivocal successes speak (grudgingly or otherwise) of working twice as hard as their male counterparts to 'just survive with dignity'.

In 2013, Amrita Solanki was posted as a sub-inspector in Rajgarh district, Madhya Pradesh. At 10 pm one night during state elections, she stopped a vehicle for a routine check. The senior election officer who was in the vehicle was affronted that she was checking an official vehicle. On the phone, Amrita tells me what happened next. 'I told him I had orders to check the vehicle. Then he started abusing me and said all kind of things. That I don't deserve this uniform. That I paid a bribe to come into the police. That I am a stupid woman and not competent to be here and that he'd immediately get me transferred. That was too much public humiliation. Besides, he insulted my uniform, which I have earned through immense hard work. Who has given men the right to discredit a woman's hard work and dignity like this? I resigned and complained in the state commission for women. Now I am going to court against him. I am determined to fight this till the end.'

Why did she resign? Amrita says that it was impossible for her to fight while still retaining her official position. Clarifying the motivation behind her resignation, she adds, 'I had to resign. Otherwise, with the uniform protocols and official responsibilities I could not have taken my fight forward. Being an on-duty officer, I could not have spoken to the media freely or could not have spoken openly against the biased departmental behaviour I faced. I resigned because I wanted to speak freely about what happened to me.' The election officer's contemptuous allegation that Amrita didn't deserve her job is fairly representative of how policewomen in India are treated. And Amrita may not be wrong in believing that she had to resign to get justice.

Take D. Padmini's case.

D. Padmini is a traffic police warden who works in the city of Kochi, Kerala. On 2 November 2013, she was on duty at a busy traffic signal near St Francis Chapel at Kathrikadavu. At 11 am, she was attacked by a man named Vinosh Varghese who suddenly got out of his car to verbally abuse her, punch her on her chest and pull off the name badge pinned to her shirt. According to a human rights agency's report on the incident, this is what happened next: 'While officially reporting the case, Ms. Padmini has met the fate of other complainants in India. The police officers first ordered her to go to the Traffic Police Station to lodge her complaint. While on her way there, she was ordered to make her report at the Kadavanthara Police Station. When she arrived at the Kadavanthara Police Station, she was ordered to make her report at the City North Police Station instead. To report a crime that occurred at 11am, the officer had to wait for three hours and was made to run between police stations.'

Twenty days later at a press conference, Padmini said that the police department did not support her in making a case against the man who attacked her. Her senior officers had summoned her four times for interrogation. In her press statement she said, 'I was hopeful of getting justice but now I realize that I won't get justice. The police thinks that I will withdraw my complaint if I am tortured. Despite the harassment, I won't withdraw my complaint as I don't want any other woman to undergo such an experience. It appears that the police are trying to frame the complainant instead of arresting the culprit.' A court had granted anticipatory bail to the man who attacked her. During the press conference, Padmini said the state police's attempts to dilute her statement had helped the accused obtain anticipatory bail.

While the stories of abuse and discrimination within the force are terrifying, as in the cases of Neetu, Sandhya and Padmini, policewomen often live through huge sexist battles at home also.

Veteran crime journalist Gyaneshwar Vatsyayan says the situation of women officers has not improved in Bihar and Jharkhand in the 30 years that he has been on the job. He adds, 'Women are still given softer beats or kept limited to women-related cases. This limits their exposure and their chances of moving ahead on the ladder. For example, the 1991 batch IPS officer Shobha Ahotkar was one of the fiercest police officers in Bihar. She was known as "Lady Hunter", the woman who took on criminals and politicians. She married an IAS officer. They had fallen in love during their training in Mussoorie, and both husband and wife were posted in the Deoghar district of undivided Bihar. One night there was a huge attack by dacoits and Shobha went in the middle of the night to investigate. When she got back home, she told me later, she had a huge fight with her husband. They actually hit each other. Her IAS husband wanted to know why she was going out to work with other men in the middle of the night!'

In Ranchi in March 2010, Inspector-General Nirmal Kaur filed a case of abuse and domestic violence against her IG husband, Amitabh Choudhry. I read the complaint filed by Nirmal Kaur (an officer in her fifties), at the women's police station of Ranchi, in which she says her husband verbally and physically abused her on different occasions. I tried to contact Nirmal Kaur several times through emails and phone calls, but she did not respond.

Yogesh Kislay, a Ranchi-based television journalist who followed the case closely, says, 'At that time I spoke to both Nirmal Kaur and her husband. While Nirmal asserted that she was being continuously mentally and physically abused by her husband, Amitabh did not comment. Insiders told me that there were severe ego problems between the couple and insecurity over Nirmal's (good) looks. But after initial reporting, the case was locally managed in the media and was immediately hushed up. A case was registered in the women's police station but no FIR was registered, and no trial took place. After a few days, Nirmal Kaur was hospitalized for a few days for psychiatric treatment (her husband tried to make out that she was mentally ill and is said to have sent her in for treatment in Ranchi). Then she was transferred to Delhi on deputation in the special police division where she now works. Despite being an IG rank officer, Nirmal could not carry her own fight through.'

In March 2013, the Home Ministry released the latest figures on the participation of women in the police force. Only 5.33 per cent of India's police force is female. Moreover, of the 15,000 police stations in the country, only 499 are all-women police stations. Despite the galloping rate of crime against women in India and the persistent demand to increase the participation of women in the police force to at least 33 per cent, the gender ratio flags miserably.

In 1933, an 18-year-old woman named C. Kamalamma put on the khaki uniform and joined the Travancore Royal Police (in what is now the state of Kerala) to become the first Indian woman to join the police force. In a television interview a few years ago, Kamalamma spoke at length about her work (as bodyguard to female members of the royal family, escorting women prisoners) and her difficulty in finding landlords who would rent their apartments to her. When she fell in love with a colleague, she was asked to leave because newly minted rules did not permit women police officers to marry. A decade and six children later, she rejoined the police force in Independent India and worked for three more decades.

Eighty years later it seems to still take a leap of faith for young women to choose to join the police. Retired additional superintendent of police (undivided Bihar), Baithnath Tiwari, certainly thinks so. He was a young sub-inspector when the first major mass recruitment of women in undivided Bihar took place in the 1970s. He says, 'In those days, exams were not taken. Women who came into the police were generally relatives of policemen and were limited to clerical office work. Whenever there was a need for a woman officer (for a raid or arrest which involved women) the station inspectors would write request letters to the headquarters. Women officers were escorted to the spot and were then dropped back. But I must say, even then, women officers were very sincere, dutiful and punctual about whatever work they were assigned. With time, policewomen really grew and came out with flying colours. But unfortunately, the police department has not matched their pace in this change.'

In February 2014 some of the changes are apparent. Far from being stuck in a Latehar-like *zenana*, at 9 pm, Inspector Shiela Toppo is still on duty, patrolling in a police jeep through a busy street of Ranchi, when I meet her. This is a routine evening patrol, part of her everyday schedule. In Toppo's career, she has investigated all kinds of crime. She has worked as a police inspector for over 25 years in different police stations across Jharkhand, including a posting as the station in-charge of Ranchi's women's police station and at the district courts.

'When I came in around 25 years ago, things were very tough,' Toppo says. 'There was stiff resistance to female cops. Nobody was ready to accept a woman working as a police officer. Young girls who are joining now are seeing an improved environment, whatever little it has improved. Maybe it's just that our male colleagues are now slowly becoming used to seeing women working with them and so the resistance has diluted a bit. But we are still not *accepted*. Men and society in general can't digest the idea of me standing by the side of a busy road in pant-shirt, with a wooden stick in my hand, walking with other male officers. They are still uncomfortable with this sight.'

While reporting from Jharkhand, I came across a number of cases involving compensatory appointments of women constables, like those of Neetu Kumar and some of her colleagues. Their situations were nearly always startling, but Ranchi-based journalist Sushil Kumar Singh had one of the strangest bits of news I'd heard.

Sushil's father was in the Bihar police force when he died in an accident. Sushil's mother was 26 and had four small children to bring up. She got a job as a police constable 'on compensatory grounds'. Every year, for 30 years, she filled a form called a 'living certificate' in order to retain her job and get her husband's pension. Sushil's mother didn't know how to read or write, so Sushil's elder brother filled the form on her behalf every year. Sushil says, 'This year, I filled it for the first time and was shocked. The living certificate stated that she was alive, *not* married and was taking care of her deceased husband's family. Women can keep their husband's pension and compensatory job only if they don't remarry for the rest of their lives. I was outraged at this medieval policy depriving women of their basic right to start a new life.'

Today, Sushil remembers his mother getting dressed and going to work every morning after finishing her daily chores at home and cooking meals for the children. He can't help the bitterness that shadows these memories, especially because he is convinced that the work destroyed her health. She's been ill for years. Sushil is particularly concerned, therefore, about the condition of widows in the police force. He says, 'The fact that widows can't marry again makes widowed women constables the most vulnerable species at any police station. Policemen know these women have heavy compensation, get pension and a salary every month. Besides, they are young. The men fight amongst themselves to emotionally and physically control these women. Once they come "under" one of these policemen, they are eternally emotionally, physically and financially exploited. This regressive policy has destructive impacts on the lives of women constables.'

We still don't have exact figures for the number of women constables in India appointed to the police in place of their husbands who died on the job. But every year, in Jharkhand and Bihar, all of these invisible officers sign 'living certificates', promising that they are unmarried and taking care of their in-laws, in return for a miserable existence.

While researching and reporting the blatant sexism in the working conditions of policewomen, I meet D.N. Gautam, former director general of police, at his residence in Patna. He starts the conversation by narrating anecdotes about the perennial lack of toilets for women in the police machinery of Bihar. He adds, 'When I was AIG-intelligence, I used to see that all women constables and officers would go to a building down the street every evening. They would go in groups, all together. I asked other male officers about where these women go. Some of them laughed and others said they didn't know. I later found that they used to go to the washroom there because our Patna Police headquarters had no toilets for women. A few years ago, when the whole office was being renovated, I gave instructions to make toilets for women on every floor. This (lack of toilets) was shocking to me, because if this was happening in Patna, you can imagine the situation in other far-away districts.'

Patna is also home to another path-breaking police officer. In Bihar's Economic Offences Wing (EOW), I meet Inspector Gauri Kumari. The DSP of the EOW, Sushil Kumar, describes her as one of the bravest officers in Bihar. He says, 'I am a '99 batch officer. After '94, the first woman candidate was selected in my batch. So the process is slow because the thinking of men has not changed. They treat women in the police like they treat women in their own home. But officers like Gauri Kumari are strong examples of what a woman police officer can do.'

Gauri Kumari was posted as a sub-inspector in the Aandar police station of Siwan district of Bihar when she was selected by the then Inspector-General (Intelligence) Rajwinder Singh Bhatti to trap the biggest don in North India, Mohammad Shahabuddin. Within a month of laying the trap, Gauri Kumari arrested Shahabuddin from his residence in Delhi in 2005. This was a daunting task that top-notch officials in Bihar had not been able to execute after trying for two years. At the time of his arrest, Shahabuddin was facing charges in more than 30 criminal cases, including eight murders and 20 attempts to murder, rioting, extortions and kidnappings. He also had non-bailable warrants issued against him in relation to the seizure and recovery of foreign firearms, ammunition and unaccounted-for foreign currency from his house in Siwan in April 2005.

I meet Gauri at DSP Sushil Kumar's chamber on the ground floor of the EOW. Recalling the arrest of Shahabuddin, Gauri says, 'I was not afraid. I did not think about any threats. We are trained to steel our minds to achieve our goals. I just had one target and that was to arrest him.' Gauri was chosen for the task because of her background—she had made a record number of arrests during her time at the Siwan police station, and her work had involved investigating criminal cases such as murders, robberies, land issues and rapes.

Unconsciously having a 'Lean In' moment, Gauri says, 'Women should work harder to carve their niche in the police department. When I used to run (for practice) on the roads of either Sivan police station campus or while chasing criminals, people would say to each other: look out, that police officer is coming. Policewomen should bring that high level of professionalism to their work so that no one can take them lightly.'

Back in early March of 2014, I went to Nizamuddin (West) market on New Delhi's Yamuna Road to meet Sheeba Aslam Fehmi. A long-time activist, Sheeba has been a member of teams involved in planning and organizing gender sensitization programmes in the Delhi and Haryana police for five years now. She has done gender sensitization programmes for the Haryana Police Academy, the Border Security Force (BSF) Academy in Tekanpur, Madhya Pradesh, and Eastern Theater (India–Bangladesh border) in West Bengal. She has also conducted gender sensitization workshops and delivered lectures at the Hyderabad-based Sardar Vallabhbhai Patel National Police Academy (around 150 IPS rank officers are trained here every year) and at the Haryana Institute of Public Administration (HIPA), which conducts research and consults in addition to training.

The kind of gender sensitization programmes organized for the different Indian forces (a mandatory part of the exhaustive training programes before joining) are usually planned and executed by a team of resource persons. This team normally includes an IPS-rank senior police official, a legal expert, a human rights expert and a social activist with expertise in gender issues such as Sheeba. Over the years, Sheeba's experience with the different forces has been varied.

Sheeba says, 'The police. They are the toughest lot. They are very explicit in their resistance towards female cops as well as women in general. For example, in every training session, I start by asking them to introduce themselves. They will give details of their dogs, children, property... everything except for their wives. I have to ask them to mention their wives. In one of my earliest training programmes in Haryana, I asked male officers to tell me what they thought about the women working with them. Most of them started laughing and then there was this buzzing in the hall—all of them complaining that women officers do nothing. When I asked them to speak to me and give me specific answers, one sub-inspector stood up and said bluntly that a women cop is "like a showpiece". He said that on tough assignments they become liabilities, as they need to be guarded and looked after. Another officer, an inspector, said that the police department does not have proper infrastructure for female staff. He complained about the lack of women's toilets and other necessary infrastructure. Most of them were of the opinion that female cops are an unnecessary burden, not worth employing.'

It is also not difficult to imagine that in a deeply patriarchal set-up, policewomen do things like harassing young couples and arresting college-going women for wearing 'fashionable' clothes and having make-up kits to feel more accepted among their peers in a deeply patriarchal work environment.

Sheeba says, 'Our research shows that 80 per cent of the women are anemic when they join the Indian police force. They are anemic and underweight. They can't run. They have never had to run. They also face discouraging remarks from their male counterparts everyday. But during the first six months of their training, these girls close the gap with tremendous zeal and energy. Later, when they start working most of these women become victims of Stockholm Syndrome and end up being protégés of other officers. At times, they resort to moral policing to feel accepted among their peers and other officers. The whole environment of police stations encourages this kind of violence.'

Sheeba says, 'The Indian police is patriarchal at its core. So, of course, the system does not focus on empowering individual women officers. Instead the women are moulded so that they are eventually and unconsciously strengthening this patriarchal set-up.'

As I leave, she says that despite all the annoyance she looks forward to conducting the next gender sensitization workshop because she still believes change is possible.

Eighty years after the first woman donned the khakhi uniform, many policewomen still have to struggle for equality and basic human dignity. Instead of empowering them with a sense of belonging within India's largest public welfare structure, the apathy and hostility of their peers, the government and society at large often places India's policewomen in a position of vulnerability. Eighty years on, women form less than 6 per cent of the police force. But despite every setback at home and at work, the Indian policewoman maintains her foothold. Every time she steps out at night on a regular patrol, she moves towards her destiny.

# 12

# Rape in West Bengal

## The land of regimental politics

SOMETIMES I SEE A WATER CANAL IN MY DREAMS. THE SOUND of water flowing through the canal and a howling woman running alongside.

I wake up with an uneasy feeling in my stomach. Every time, after this dream, I have tried to remember more details about this water canal. Where have I seen this? And before I am able to even properly open my eyes, my mind transports me to the outskirts of the Bardhaman district of West Bengal. A small figment of memory takes me back.

Of course, I have seen this particular water canal. It's not only a dream. I have been here twice. Once on the last day of 2014 and then again in July 2016.

On the morning of 27 October 2013, a 17-year-old-girl was found dead in this canal. Her family had been searching with mounting desperation for her since the past two days and when she was finally found, they could not gather the courage to look at her.

Her body was found half-naked, lying by the flowing water of the canal. She had been slit from different points and there were deep blade marks slashed all over, as if 'someone had peeled her skin off like we peel onions at home', her mother had told me later during an interview. There were nibbling marks around her breasts and deep bite marks around her neck. The post-mortem report says that there is clear evidence of forced intercourse attempted multiple times. Her vagina was torn apart and broken pieces of plastic and glass bottles were found inside her private parts. There were marks of strangulation around her neck. The post-mortem report mentions the presence of bluish and reddish spots all over her body which implies sexual and physical harm. It also says that the girl was asphyxiated to death hours before she was thrown in the stream of water.

The day before her pink rubber slippers, her umbrella and her pink Ladybird cycle were found near the same stream. The family was devastated. The police were informed . But they said, '*Dhoondho-dhoondho* (look for her yourself)'. After 24 hours the family found the girl's body at the same spot where her cycle and other belongings were found a day before. They informed the police again. This time the cops came 'to collect the dead body for post-mortem'.

I will get into the details of the crime and the 'why' and the 'how' and the 'where' of it later in this chapter but first I want you to know that this is a lower middle class couple whose lives have been bordering on extreme poverty for as long as they can remember. The husband drives trucks all over the highways in the country to make a living for the family. The wife stayed at home raising her two kids. A 16-year-old son who is alive and a 17-year-old daughter who is now dead. The family belongs to a religious minority and lives in a one-room house which they had been able to construct only recently in the face of immense financial difficulties. The son is a 'kind human', but he was never into studies, the mother told me.

The family showed me an entrance examination admit-card that came by post after the girl died in October 2013. She was only 17 but wanted to be financially independent as soon as possible. She was to write a paper for becoming a Ticket Collector (TT) in Indian railways in December—two months after she was brutally gang-raped and killed.

The parents thought of their daughter as not being different from their son in any way. They braved huge opposition from their relatives and friends when they decided to educate the daughter. But the truck driver father had felt a spark in his daughter early on. He believed that she had an 'unusual eagerness for education and that she really wanted to make something of herself since she was a kid'.

The father wanted to do everything to provide her a chance to study and fly!

The parents loved their daughter dearly. She was their only hope.

~

I am on on the outskirts of Bardhaman town of West Bengal. It's around 24 hours and 1400 kilometres away from Delhi by road. It's the last day of December in the year 2014. A cool breeze brushes against my cheeks as I finish my long journey from Delhi and finally reach this lower middle class settlement situated around six kilometres away from the Bardhaman district headquarters.

Hanging on the periphery like a shadow of the real Bardhaman town, this area comes under the urban municipality governance system. But the settlement lacks basic facilities like proper roads, streets lights and uninterrupted power supply.

I start walking alongside the canal and reach the spot

where her cycle, her umbrella, her slippers and later on her dead body was discovered. I stand there and look around. There is pin drop silence, except for the sound of a drill machine coming from a nearby construction site, running through my mind as a constantly irritating background score.

The girl's house is barely 200 metres away from the spot where her lifeless body was found in October 2013. Just across the muddy approach road next to the canal. As I walk into this working class neighbourhood for the first time in December 2014, I am told that she was the only kid in this whole *mohalla* who could write and speak fluently in English.

A neighbour who is also a witness in the case, starts sobbing while walking me up to the victim's house from the canal. 'She would speak so fast in English and we all would look at her face in awe. And she could speak and write Hindi and Bengali as well,' she said and wiped her tears with her printed cotton dupatta. 'She wanted to work and earn money so that her father could stop risking his life on the highways driving huge luggage carriers every night.'

Neighbours remember the victim as a happy, hard-working, compassionate and kind child. Women who lived around the victim's house knew that the girl had also planned to fill forms for joining the police force as a back-up plan. 'She used to say this all the time I remember: "Didi, I will pass railway recruitment board exams. But god-forbid, if I fail, I will try police force. But I will get a job as soon as I finish school." She had a single-minded focus. To get a job and support her family and that too at such a young age,' said another woman who lived next door to the victim's family.

~

It was around noon when I first entered the victim's house.

The victim's younger brother ran in and suddenly disappeared in a corner of the house. He came back after a few minutes, his hands full with a couple of small trophies and some documents. 'She stood second in the various activities and competitions conducted during her NCC training,' was the first thing he said to me while handing over a Bengal National Cadet Corps (NCC) trophy won by his elder sister to me.

At the victim's house I looked at all the *material* that her family had kept in front of me. Everything spread out on the floor was related to her—pieces of her life and memories dear to her family.

There was her English notebook lying in between the stacks of her school books. I picked it up slowly and turned the cover. She had drawn two flowers and a flying bird alongside her name on the front page of the copy. I looked at the flowers and the bird and I touched them. Then I lifted the copy up in my hands and tried to smell it.

Though I didn't know the girl I wanted to know if her copies still smelled of her fingers. They didn't. It was over a year since she passed away and her copies then had a stale smell.

I then tried to turn the first page over slowly to take a look inside the living years of this girl frozen in time in her 17th year.

My fingers started shaking. Is anyone ever ready to look this deep into the lives of the dead? Especially the dead who died an undeserving, unjustifiable, cruel, unfortunate death? I felt a crunch in my stomach. A sinking feeling. My head was dizzy for a second and I started sweating in the cold of December.

I felt as if I was a metal coin dropped from a ship—sinking

slowly. I could feel myself slowly free-falling towards the ocean bed in that moment. Perhaps I did not have the courage for this. I stepped outside the house for a moment to control my tears. I wanted to howl my head off at that moment. But instead I closed my eyes, clinched both my fists and tried to hold myself together.

As I opened my eyes, I found the brother of the victim standing in front of me.

'Are you okay?' he asked.

I could see the canal behind the victim's brother and could hear sounds of running water overlapping his question. He was the first one to discover his sister's body. Later during the day, he told me that he just shouted '*Mil gayi* (found her)' for everyone searching around to know that she was found. After that he sat down where he was standing. He kept his hand on his head and started sobbing. 'I had not seen anything that gross and mutilated ever in my life. I think my heart stopped beating. I couldn't believe this is my sister lying in front of me.'

'I am okay,' I said, and we both walked in.

~

I was sitting on the floor of the small covered varanda inside the victim's house now.

I remember holding her notebooks, her railway recruitment board entrance admit-cards, a photocopy of the FIR and her post-mortem report in a single bunch of documents in one hand. Later, I kept them one below another in a straight sequence laid out on the floor.

The NNC trophies, the English notebooks with a detailed analysis of a poem on 'freedom' written by the girl on the first page, the entrance admit-cards, the FIR, the post-mortem reports, passport- and postcard-size pictures of the girl—all lay together on the floor. I kept looking at the collage that I had created for a couple of minutes.

The unlettered mother of the victim used to keep a record of her marksheets and her various certificates of excellence in a separate plastic folder. Now she keeps copies of her daughter's post-mortem reports, FIR and all other case-related documents in the same folder.

~

If you put 'West Bengal', 'Rape' and 'Data' as key words in Google search, you will get a number of news stories with screaming headlines saying things like 'Crime against women at alarming levels in Bengal', 'Bengal is most unsafe for women shows latest data' and 'Bengal ranks first/second/third in crime against women'. If you click on those links, you will get to know that West Bengal has been topping the charts of crime against women in India for a couple of years now. Whenever the National Crime Records Bureau comes up with its annual figures about the status of crime in the country, the name of West Bengal comes and goes as a recurring theme in the matter of 'crime against women data'. Since the beginning of this decade, the state has been rotating ranks in the top four positions of states having highest rates of crime against women in India. Rapes and trafficking constitute a large part of these figures.

While researching for this book, the high figures of crime against women in West Bengal struck me as surprising. Because I didn't remember coming across too many news stories related to violence against women in Bengal in newspapers. Also, as a North Indian—with limited knowledge of West Bengal—I always thought of the state as one where people are culturally richer and better-read than their North Indian counterparts.

Whenever I would think of Bengal I would think of Satyajit Ray's cinema, Rabindranath Tagore's poetry and people reading in a library or singing on the streets. I would think of beautiful Bengali women with big Durga eyes and long hair. I would think of Mahashewta Devi, the left politics and *Hazaar Chaurasi ki Maa*. I would think of the regimental political fight between the Communist Party of India (Marxist) or CPI(M) and the All India Trinamool Congress (TMC). The CPI(M) ruled the state for more than 34 years and TMC's Mamata Banerjee had taken over from them in May 2011. Left parties project themselves as the flag-bearers of equality between genders and talk a lot about women empowerment and in case of TMC, Mamata herself was the first woman chief minister of the state. So ideally, the situation of women should be better here, I thought.

But the figures were telling a different story. As a reporter who has lived and worked mostly in North India, I felt both intrigued and limited by my knowledge of the state. The internet was not of much help because most of the original journalism happening in Bengal was being published in Bengali. There are English newspapers also running and doing well in Bengal but they are few in number and cannot match the grip of local language papers on readers. But I was curious and wanted to try and find out what's happening on the ground.

Just then a spat of major rape cases coming out of Bengal shocked the whole nation. The 2012 Suzette Jordan rape case, the 2013 Kamduni rape case, the 2014 Birbhum rape case and the 2014 Madhyamgram rape case, to name a few.

Along with this, shocking statements of the incumbent chief minister, Mamata Banerjee, referring to rape victims as 'liars' who are making false allegations to 'bring bad name' to the Government of West Bengal led to international outrage. Soon, other elected representatives from the TMC like Kakoli Ghosh Dastidar, started dismissing rape survivors and painted everyone who complained of sexual assault as 'conspiring against the government' and 'trying to defame' the TMC's governance. This ostrich approach of Mamata Banerjee's government attracted lot of flak from media and elsewhere but the previous Left governments were no better either.

## Dislocation of rape victims

By the end of 2014 I was preparing for my reporting trip to West Bengal. I was calling up lots of people and trying to line up my stories like reporters have to. I zeroed in on the cases of rape and sexual assault that took place during the 2007 Nandigram violence. The state was ruled by the CPI(M) then.

In Delhi, most people in routine civilian lives know of the Left politics through their student wings—Student Federation of India (SFI) and All India Student's Association (AISA). The parent parties have little relevance in India's mainstream politics now, but their student wings keep storming back to headlines here in the capital. They often hold protests on issues of public interest here at Jantar Mantar. Protesting against violence and crimes happening to women forms a large part of the left student politics in Delhi.

Back to my reporting trip prep in November 2014—I called and called and called. I reached out to the best sources and the best reporters in the state, worked for over weeks on this. But, to my surprise, nobody was able to put me in touch with even one family which suffered sexual abuse during the Nandigram violence.

The stringers and local reporters backed off. I was

informed through highly placed sources that 'the victims do not live in their original residences anymore'. They have been re-located and no one knows that new location. I was told that the families have been under 'immense pressure to not speak to the media' because it will bring a 'bad name' to the political party that was ruling the state in 2007.

After that I tried to meet the Kamduni and Madhyamgram families. And the same story was repeated. The families have been relocated temporarily and no one knows where they are living now! These rape cases happened in the TMC regime. I heard similar accounts on the lines of being 'pressurized by the government to not speak to the media'. Because 'these fabricated stories' will, as the first woman chief minister of the state has indicated before, 'bring bad name to the government'.

In my reporting career of six years, this was a first. This was the first time I was not able to trace a victim's family. This was the first time I was not able to locate where the family lives. West Bengal was tougher than even Haryana or Rajasthan—which are normally considered to be difficult states to report on gender violence.

I was able to find and reach out to the victim's family in Bardhaman. I will go back to the story which I have been telling you in this chapter in a bit. But I also wanted to understand why I was not able to have access to victim families of major rape cases from Bengal.

Was it political witch-hunting? Is political pressure being used to suppress the voices of rape victims in Bengal instead of supporting them?

I wanted answers to these questions.

On the evening of 30 December 2014, I met Swati Bhattacharjee in her office in Kolkata. Swati, who works as a senior assistant editor at *Ananda Bazar Patrika*, has edited a book of essays on sexual violence in India. She has also extensively written and reported on crime against women in West Bengal.

Talking about the new spate of brutal rapes and murders in West Bengal, she said that there is a certain kind of cultural revivalism taking place in Bengal. 'As women are being more educated and achieving an elevated standard of life, organized crime against them is increasing. Rapes and murders by strangers are on the rise and there is a stress of physical submission of the victim in these cases. The kind of violence happening shows that there is a sentiment of "putting a woman in her place" in society. It reflects on "just a slight twist" in the patriarchal consciousness of the people of the state. They want to benefit from the empowerment of women, but want to keep the final control of their lives with themselves.'

Swati feels that the bitter tooth and nail political battle between the Left and TMC often blinds them towards social and gender issues. 'Mamata received a lot of criticism for her statements on rape victims and rightly so. But she has also done a couple of good things in the state for survivors of sexual assault. For example, she has opened a number of fast track courts, a number of police stations manned only by women, etc. West Bengal has got India's first all women's court as well. And if something happens to you, you can go to the police station and get an FIR filed. Earlier, in the Left regime, it was not possible for a rape victim to get a complaint registered easily. So that way things have improved a bit. But the Left is a highly regimental party. They have top to bottom communication system and no one deviates from it. Mamata, on the other hand, could not handle the communication part very well. She, as well as her MPs, went on to give silly statements on crime against women—which will prove to be damaging for her own political image in the long run.'

Swati agrees that rape victims face a certain political pressure to 'keep quiet' in Bengal and feels that the women here are the first victims of the rising crimes in politics. She adds, 'There is a general rise in the criminalization of politics in Bengal and women are the first victims. Secondly, politicians who are giving irresponsible statements against women are not being held accountable for their deeds. This further encourages sexist behaviour at a higher leadership level while the party's foot soldiers working in small villages also feel that they will be shielded by the state. They feel they can do whatever they want with women and get away with it.'

≈

Back to Bardhaman for the second time. The list of the accused in the Bardhaman canal rape case mirrors Swati's sentiments.

It's July 2016 and this is my second reporting trip to Bardhaman.

I meet the victim's mother—who's in her early 40s—as she stands at the main entrance of her house. She is wearing a printed green cotton gown and has covered her head using a red cotton dupatta.

The first thing she tells me is a devastating piece of news. 'At the time of filing the FIR, they had booked 11 men. Later, as the investigation progressed, they filed a chargesheet against eight of them. But not even one among the eight was punished. The special Bardhaman court recently let off all eight accused in the case of my daughter's rape and murder,' she says as both of us stand outside her house.

We look at each other with blank eyes. The canal is still flowing on the right side of the house and I can still hear the sound of water flowing through it.

≈

As we settle down for an interview, the victim's mother—surprised and anguished by the trial court verdict—recounts the whole sequence of events.

'My daughter loved to study. She would go to school every day and then attend her tuitions religiously. Even if it would be raining and I would ask her to skip her classes, she would say: "Mummy, I will not bunk my class." She went to tuition like every other day on the evening of 25 October 2013. She normally came back home by 9 pm latest. But that day it was raining heavily. When she did not return by 9 pm, I thought she might have stayed back at my sister's place, who lives very near to her tuition class. I thought that was the obvious thing to do as it was raining heavily. I called my daughter and then my sister to confirm. But neither's phone was getting connected. My son and I thought the signals are bad because of the rain. We were worried but we believed our gut instinct and tried to sleep. The rain did not stop the whole night. Next morning, when I called my sister, I got to know that my daughter is not at her house. I got extremely worried. Her father was in Assam at that time, driving a truck. I froze. I couldn't think coherently. Then my neighbours and relatives came to help. We filed a missing complaint at the police station and started looking for her ourselves. The police did not co-operate.'

The mother informed the police that a bunch of unemployed men used to eve-tease her daughter on her way to the tuition. They were all minions of the local TMC leader so the family was scared of complaining against them. 'My daughter told me that there is this bunch of men who drink and gamble in an under-construction building on her way to the tuition class. They used to pass comments on her and say things like: "*Kya maal ja rahi hai* (Look, what an attractive woman is passing by)." I asked her to change her route but there was no other route. I asked her to keep quiet. But she was a young and angry girl. One day she snapped back at the men and said that she will complain to the police. That day, when she came home and told me what has happened—I was very scared. We knew that those boys are under the local TMC guy's protection. So we went to him—the local TMC party worker from our mohalla. I begged in front of him with folded hands. I begged him to control those boys. My husband was not in town and I was scared of taking the case to the police. I was scared that there will be repercussions on my daughter and I had no confidence in the police. There were repercussions anyway. The TMC guy warned those men to stay away from my daughter. Obviously they did not listen to him and thought how dare we complain against them. Next day, my daughter was kidnapped. Two days later we found her body slashed—slit from everywhere. She was found naked lying in the canal. Her private parts were looking like a pound of open-cut flesh. They had chewed down her breasts and bitten her body like dogs. Eleven men were booked and later eight chargesheeted. When I try to imagine—a little child being thrashed down by around a dozen men—I feel like killing myself. They raped her till her body degenerated'... the mother kept talking... words and tears flowing simultaneously.

'Our lawyer did not inform us anything about the judgment day. When we heard our neighbours saying that the accused in our case have been acquitted—we felt shocked. My daughter's father and I went running to our lawyer. We both kept crying throughout. The lawyer said that there were no witnesses from our side that's why we we lost the case. There were no evidence to support our case.'

There were nine witnesses from the victim's side but all

of them had turned hostile. 'Even my neighbours could not stand by me. Everyone got threats. The accused were related to TMC members. Witnesses were told that their children will be killed if they opened their mouths in the court. There was an attack on my house as well. Last year, some men tried to put my house on fire when we were asleep. We have reported the case to the police but nothing happened. There was so much evidence—my daughter's cycle and umbrella and slippers were recovered from the canal. I don't know what the police did with the evidence. And witnesses? If the police are not able to protect the witnesses, is that our fault?' she asks.

The parents have been advised by well-wishers—and threatened by families of the accused—to leave this area and settle down somewhere else. But the father refused to leave.

'He loved his daughter more than his son. He refused to leave and said if my daughter is buried here... I will also get buried here... next to her.'

As we sit together and wade through the old pictures of the 17-year-old victim, the mother keeps talking and crying at the same time. I take pictures of all case-related documents silently and keep listening to her. There comes a point when she starts talking to herself—words and tears flowing out together. 'We have no money and we are poor. So the government lawyer we got, treated us like we do not exist. He did not even inform us the day when our judgment was supposed to be pronounced. The judge? She was a woman. When I told her that the rapists had inserted broken pieces of glass in my daughter's vagina, she said, "I am not sitting here to listen to your melodrama". Was I doing drama in court? Is the murder and gang-rape of my child a drama? The whole country stood up for the Delhi bus rape victim. Everyone here stood up for the Kamduni rape victim. But no one said anything when all those accused

in my daughter's case were acquitted! They were all jealous
of her because she was smart and beautiful. She could speak
English and she was going to be a big person one day... that
is why those men raped and killed her. My son has left his
studies. He says that his sister was killed because she was good
in studies and because she wanted to study more. From the
day he discovered his sister's body by the canal, he has gone
into depression.'

The girl's mother believes that her daughter was gang-
raped and killed because she was making the men around
her insecure. She was fearless, confident, hard-working and
intelligent. She was going to write competitive exams and was
on the brink of starting a new independent life for herself. She,
and her whole existence, was 'odd' in the small neighbourhood
hanging on the edges of Bardhaman district. In an ideal
world, this oddity should have been welcomed, encouraged
and nurtured. But here, in the outskirts of Bardhaman town,
it fueled the sense of urgency in men around her 'to put her
in her place'.

The death of justice is always darker than the death
of a human being. It's the final defeat of democracy, the
Constitution and the kindness of the human spirit. 'If the
eight accused have been acquitted, then who killed and gang-
raped my daughter. Someone did for sure. The post-mortem
report says that she was raped multiple times. She was killed.
I buried her with my own hands. Who killed her? Who raped
her?' asks the mother.

I take a passport sized picture of the girl from her mother
and keep it in my wallet. There was something about that
picture which held me by the gut—I keep looking at that
picture often. Her deep large eyes. The compassionate smile on
her face. Her long hair neatly braided and tied with a ribbon.

This was the first picture she had got clicked for using to fill entrance exam forms. There is so much hope in that face; it makes me kneel down.

That face deserves an answer. The mother deserves an answer. The body lying by the canal deserves an answer. The devastated father and the young brother who dropped out of school deserve answers.

Who killed this child of god?

## Postscript

The parents have decided to continue the case and fight for justice in the Kolkata High Court. They said they will continue to fight till they get an answer. Who raped and killed their daughter? They (still) want justice.

# 13

# The Question of Rehabilitation of Rape Survivors in India

## Policy and ground realities

THE BOY AIMED A STROKE WITH HIS OLD CRANKY WOODEN BAT and strongly hit the stale rubber ball, rushing through the air towards him under that sweltering June summer sky. As the ball stormed out of the boundaries of that small pebbled dusty playground situated in the centre of a distant lesser known village in the Sonipat district of Haryana, children happily started chanting, 'Sixer! Sixer!' I stood quietly on the periphery of the playground and waited patiently for the next few minutes till the celebrations calmed down. Then waved my hand up in the air and interrupted their game by calling out for help.

It was the summer of 2013 and I was standing in the Atail-Idana village which falls in the Gohana tehsil of Sonipat. I remember watching a child batsman walking towards me as his friends looked on. He must have been around 13 years old. When I asked for directions to Sunil's house in *Dhanak mohalla* of the village, he broke into a suggestive smile and exchanged a quick grin with his team players. Then he quickly left his bat on the ground and walked me across the playground, to a house situated in a corner at the end towards north of the playground. 'Sunil and his parents are not at home. The door will be opened only if one of us, among his relatives, knocks,' he tell me on our way while panting for a steady breath. '*Darwaja kholo ri, janaani aayin hain* (Get the door opened, a lady is here),' he shouts while banging on the door.

When the black wooden door slowly opened after a while, two little girls peeped out, quickly let me in the house and immediately closed the door on my back. They were both around 12 years old. There was a semi-concrete courtyard in front of this main entrance and two buffaloes were tied at the courtyard's peripheral boundary. Behind it was a washing area where a young woman was washing clothes by the side of a hand pump.

A small one room house with a staircase leading to a small open terrace stood empty beyond her. This young woman who was washing clothes by the hand pump was Sunil's 20-year-old wife, Ragini. Her face was covered with a dupatta as she scrubbed the collar of a pale shirt with a cheap detergent soap. The girls who opened the door for me were Ragini's 'family sentinels'. Since 28 September 2012, Ragini's in-laws have been keeping a close watch on her. She was not allowed to talk to anyone. She could not answer the door nor could she receive a phone call if the mobile rang. Even if it is too hot inside the one-room house, she is not permitted to sit outside in the courtyard. Since there were no toilets in the house, every time she had to go out in the fields to relive herself, she had to take someone from her family along with her—because no one at home trusts her at all. In fact, her family members literally hate to even look at her face.

But Ragini's life was not always like this. A Class 5 school dropout, she helped her mother in household chores as an adolescent. Then she got married to Sunil in 2012 and like any other 19-year-old bride, she dreamt of a beautiful life with her husband, whom she said she loved very much.

But a horrific incident turned her life upside down. On 28 September 2012, Ragini was kidnapped and then gang-raped by four men for five days and four nights across three different cities and small towns of Haryana.

With her undying courage and bravery, she did finally manage to escape the clutches of her rapists. But while getting away, she had no idea that her real ordeal had only begun now. While running away from her rapists on that humid September night, she had thought that she was running towards the protection and safety of her family and the law. She had no idea that in this part of the world if women run away from the hands of their rapists, they always walk into a completely changed world. A world where she would be called a whore, a thief and a woman without character for the rest of her life because of a crime that actually happened to her. She had no idea that justice and a dignified life would be denied to her not only by her family but also by the Indian Courts. Despite being the victim, she was bearing the brunt of familial and judicial neglect. Her story is a testament to everything that is wrong with the Indian judicial system when it comes to rapes. Moreover, her story paints a distressing picture of the bleak future of victims of sexual violence in both legal and societal frameworks in India. To put the question of 'Rehabilitation of Rape Victims' in India in context, it is important to first go through Ragini's story.

Ragini's husband Sunil sells utensils and her father-in-law works as a vendor in the village market. Both were not at home on the day I visited her in Haryana.

Allowing me in her single-room house, Ragini tries to send the two little 'guards girls' away by engaging them in the task of 'bringing *chai-patti* (tea leaves) from a nearby shop'. She whispers, 'I must send them away, or they will tell my mother-in-law everything and then I will be in trouble. They always leave these girls back home to spy on my movements.'

It was around 1 pm and all of us were suffering under the sweltering intense heat of peak summer made worse by North Indian heat waves. After sending her family guards away, Ragini settled down on a small wooden bed for a conversation with me. She was wearing a thick polyester golden brown '*Anarkali salwar kameez*' in that boiling summer afternoon. But her veil was up now, covering only her hair. As we exchanged our first few silent glances, I took her hand in mine and urged her to tell me whatever was there in her heart. We both kept quiet for the next 10 minutes. When I again requested her to share her story, she looked into my eyes and started crying and then slowly opened up saying, 'I only wish to die now, didi. I would have killed myself long ago. But these people won't let me die. They never leave me alone even for a moment so that I can kill myself. See, I am so helpless that I can't even kill myself.'

~

In September 2012, Ragini had gone to visit her parents for the first time after her marriage. Her parents belong to the Dhanuk community of Harayana which is traditionally associated with jobs like grass cutting, cleaning and tending to animals. Dhanuk is a sub caste listed under the scheduled castes category in India and they have been traditionally doing all of the above listed work for the upper-caste landlords of Harayna as bounded labourers... tending their animals...

growing their crops. Like all scheduled caste families, Ragini's house was also situated at the furthermost end of her village named Banwasa, also situated in the Gohana tehsil of Sonipat district.

Ragini's parents work as bonded labourers and looked after buffaloes of upper-caste Jat families on leases. On an equally hot summer day in June 2013, sitting in her one room semi-concrete house, I met Ragini's mother Suman, who kept on scratching the mud floor with the torn corner of her old printed sari, a futile gesture that gave vent to her sense of helplessness. After a few minutes of silence she told me, 'We had saved money for years to marry off our daughter, which we did... and with lots of love. And then she came back for her first visit to us after her marriage. The next day four boys kidnapped her from the railway-crossing near our village. She returned home after five days in a physically torn and mentally devastated condition. We wanted all the culprits to be punished so we even reported our case to the police. But then the villagers and our community started putting pressure on us. As time passed, our society's pressure started becoming stronger. We did stand up to them for a while but after a point, we had no option but to withdraw the complaint.'

This incident happened in the same month of September 2012 when 20 other rape cases were reported back to back in Haryana and the state suddenly grabbed national headlines for the alarming rise in cases of sexual violence against women.

Back in Atail-Idana village, Ragini adds, 'I had a neighbour in my maternal village Banwasa. Her name was Maphi and she used to own a beauty-parlour in our neighborhood. She also taught me sewing. We were friends. On 28 September, she told me that my husband had come from Atail-Idana and had sent a message for me that he wanted to meet me at the railway crossing near Banwasa village. I believed her but when I went to meet my husband, he was not there.'

Instead, she was kidnapped by two men at the railway crossing locally known as *Gohana Phatak*. Ragini alleges that two men named Sanjay and Sunil forcefully picked her up in a white car from the railway crossing on that fateful afternoon. Then they took her to an isolated room in the middle of a rice-field on Gohana-Khakrohi Road. But here two other men were already present—they were Anil from Ahmedpur Majra and Shravan from Hitadi, she tells me. She further adds, 'I was forcefully made to sniff something that made me unconscious. When I regained consciousness, I was lying in a room that housed a water pump situated in the middle of an open field. Those four men... they were all over me, biting and pinching me. They watched dirty videos on their mobiles, laughed and clawed at me. I was without clothes for four days. Then they took me to Kurukshetra town and from there to Panipat. I was wearing some jewellery that I had received on my wedding from my mother—a pair of gold ear-rings, a pair of silver anklets and a golden finger ring. They sold everything and handed me an old... torn *salwar kameez* to wear. I begged them to leave me, but each time they only laughed at me. Somehow, one night I got an opportunity to escape and I secretly phoned my father. The police came to rescue me. But by then, five days had already passed.'

Ragini and her family had initially claimed that Maphi was also involved in the crime, but they had to get her released themselves. Suman further told me, 'After we reported the incident to the police, we came to know that all the four boys were from our own *Dhanak* community. For the first three months the villagers supported us. They insisted that we should get Maphi released as she is the daughter-in-law of the village, while the four boys should stay in jail. It became a matter of the honour for the village and we were pressurized from all sides. As a result, we had to withdraw our statement against Maphi. After this, we were pressurized to do the same for the four accused boys as well! For a whole 10 days, people from our community would come and sit right outside my door. The old men from the accused boys' families also used to come and pressurize us. They were saying that they will boycott us from the village if we did not take our complaint back. Soon after, Ragini's in-laws came too. They said that their son's life was being threatened by the accused boys' families. Ragini is a girl, we cannot get her married again. And her in-laws might not have taken her back if we had not backed out from the court case. So we were forced to withdraw all the charges.'

During the interview Ragini agreed to her mother's statements and added, 'I was helpless. My in-laws felt that if I pursued the case, it would bring disgrace to them and their family. My husband's life was also in danger. Everyone said that if I wanted my in-laws to accept me again, I should change my statement before the court and say that I was not raped, that during those five days I was at my in-laws' place. I was told to state that the medical reports of my rape came positive because I had sex with my husband during those days. I had to do what I was told to do. Everyone from my village was present there in the court room. I couldn't speak the truth as they would all have disowned me forever... or might even have killed me and my husband.'

On 24 April 2013, additional district and sessions judge, Manisha Batra, sentenced Ragini to 10 days in jail and a fine of Rs 500 under perjury for giving a false statement in the court in Sonipat.

I interviewed the vice-president of the All India Women's

Democratic Assosiation, Jagmati Sangvan, after interviewing Ragini and her family in Haryana. Jagmati called Ragini's story a tragic example of the societal pressure put on rape victims in the absolute absence of rehabilitation policies. She said, 'It is one of the most heinous rape incidents. Even the judiciary could not see that the girl was under pressure and passed the verdict against her. Clearly, the ground reality is that even the new laws have failed to give justice to women.'

Meanwhile, Ragini's nightmare continued. When I asked her to consider lodging a complaint with the police, she said, 'There is no question of it. Everybody here believes that I am guilty. They say that I actually knew those men and had run off with them to have fun. Even if I comb my hair or sit in the courtyard, my young sister-in-law and brother-in-law pass comments like "Who are you inviting now? Aren't you satisfied yet?" They call me vulgar and cheap. My mother-in-law taunts me for not bearing children. Even my husband doesn't understand me and the violence I went through. He also believes that I ran away willingly. I can't even breathe and you are talking of going to the police! What was my fault? I would want to see those criminals get a heavy punishment. But it's not in my hands. I am supposed to stay silent. So I am staying silent.'

## Rape in India

With a 902% increase from 1971 to 2012, rape is undoubtedly the fastest growing crime in India.[1] An analysis of the figures given out every year by the National Crime Records Bureau (NCRB) of India puts out a grim picture. The number of registered rape cases in India has shot up from 2,919 in 1973 to 24,206 in 2011 while the conviction rate has dropped by

18 per cent.[2] Recently, India has seen a huge surge in debate
on the question of rapes and violence against women. On 16
December 2012, a young medical student was gang-raped,
beaten, slashed with iron rods and then left to die on the
roads of Delhi in a brutally battered state along with her male
companion. Now known as the 'Delhi December gang-rape
case', the sheer violence, cruelty and decline of basic human
values reflected in all segments of Indian society involved
in this case, shocked India. The country immediately saw a
phenomenal uprising and mass mobilization against sexual
violence, specifically, rapes in India. Since then, there has been
a lot of noise around sexual violence in India. People have
come out on the streets to protest and there is a consistent
demand to ensure the safety of women in India.

## Justice Verma Committee Report 2013

Responding to the nationwide protests, the Government of
India constituted a committee under the chairmanship of
the late Justice J.S. Verma to 'recommend amendments in
criminal law for quicker trial and enhanced punishments for
sexual assault against women'.[3] With Ex-Solicitor General
Gopal Subramanian and former Justice Leila Seth in his team,
Justice Verma reviewed over 70,000 suggestions sent to the
Verma Committee by members of civil society, lawmakers,
non-governmental organizations and general public through
post, fax and emails. The committee came up with a landmark
report spanning over 600 pages within 29 days. Considered
as one of the most radical, progressive, fiercely humane,
compassionate report and pro-women in its texture, this
white paper was released on 23 January 2013. The report had
comprehensive recommendations on laws related to sexual

violence, child sexual abuse, human trafficking, medical examinations of victims and it vouched heavily for sensitizing the police, electorate, educational sectors and people in general about handling the problem of crime against women.

## The Criminal Law Amendment Act 2013

The Justice Verma Committee Report was welcomed and warmly received as experts interpreted it as 'a moment of triumph'[4] in the history of the Indian women's movement. The essence of the Verma Committee Report was that it holds the state responsible for the condition of women in the country and calls for motivated changes in priorities of governance. Among the most significant recommendations of the Committee was a 'Bill of Rights' for women wherein the state shall commit itself to provide right to life, security, and bodily integrity; democratic and civil rights; equality and non-discrimination; right to secured spaces; special provisions for elderly and disabled women; and protection of women in distress.[5]

Considering that crime against women cannot be wiped out overnight, the Verma Committee, emphasized on the need to develop a more effective response care system for rape and sexual assault victims in its recommendations. The United Nations also urged the Government of India to implement the recommendations of this committee in spirit and letter. But when the Criminal Law Amendment Ordinance 2013 came out in February 2013, it had no provisions for the rehabilitations of rape victims as such. The ordinance was also heavily criticized by civil society for skipping some major recommendations of the Justice Verma Committee Report like 'recognition of marital rape, new provisions on the offence of breach of command responsibility, non-requirement of sanction for prosecuting members of the security forces accused of sexual assault and rape, and provision for trying them under ordinary criminal laws for sexual crimes.'[6]

Also, the ordinance was criticized by women's rights groups in India for bypassing crucial recommendations on 'reforms in constitution, governance, policing and education' and for 'not recognizing the rehabilitation of rape survivors as responsibility of the state'. The ordinance failed to provide for rehabilitation of victims/survivors by the state, thereby continued with the faulty approach where rapes and acid attacks are viewed as matters between individuals rather than a general phenomenon and the state's responsibility.[7] Though the ordinance was quickly passed and the Criminal Law Amendment Act 2013 came into effect in India from March 2013, the debate on the ordinance in Parliament was partially considered patriarchal[8] in its tone as it ignored rape victims' care and focused mostly on defining rape and punishing sex crimes.[9]

## Why is rehabilitation of rape victims in India important?

Before coming to 'the present rehabilitation policies available for rape victims in India' and 'the ground realities of those policies', I want to discuss the importance of rehabilitation of rape victims in India.

Along with quick retributive justice, compensatory rehabilitation is important for victims of all crimes but it is especially more important when it comes to rape in the Indian context. This is because rape is the only crime in India for which the victim is blamed. Huge public shame and social stigma attached with the crime has already been keeping women away from reporting rapes since ages. As the fact goes, against every reported rape case in India, at least 30 go unreported because of fear and shame.[10] Shame of losing one's family, job, friends, social circle and most importantly, the fear of losing one's self-respect, keeps women away from reporting rape at police stations. Everyone—right from the family, friends, to the police—views the victim with doubt. Her testimony is dismissed by throwing random questions on her character. In a situation such as this, with little or no help extended from the legal and administrative infrastructure, most women either choose to stay silent or back out from their complaints, like Ragini did. Rehabilitation policies are important to instil confidence in Indian women to make them believe that they can have a life after rape. Good rehabilitation policies and effective retributive justice will encourage women to come out and file complaints. A comprehensive rape rehabilitation policy will help an Indian woman in trusting her state enough to come out and fearlessly report against the violation she suffered.

In early August 2013, a bench of Justices R.M. Lodha and Madan B. Lokur of the Supreme Court of India also came out strongly in favour of putting in place an 'adequate compensation and rehabilitation scheme for rape victims' for the lifelong ordeal they had to undergo. The bench added, 'No amount of money can restore the dignity and confidence of rape victims. However, certain measures such as adequate compensation, insurance, employment and social security schemes may help in rehabilitating the rape victims to a certain extent.'[11]

Highlighting the importance of interim compensation and rehabilitation, Brijesh Kalappa, advocate in the Supreme Court of India and additional advocate general of Haryana said in an

interview that a change in rape laws has been rightly brought
into effect by the Parliament through the Criminal Law
(Amendment) Act, 2013 because 'it was timely to demonstrate
how important women are and that the Government is
serious'. Provisions for compensation were also inserted in
the Criminal Procedure Code in 2009 to provide for interim
compensation the moment an FIR is lodged. The idea is to
help the survivor sustain herself during trial. 'Once the trial
is over, the court will take care of the victim's requirement
while passing an appropriate order. Interim compensation
is to help the victim keep up the fight and aid the cause of
justice; otherwise, the victim may give up and the whole case
will collapse,' Kalappa added.[12]

## Scheme for the relief and rehabilitation of victims of rape

Ironically, only one scheme (not law) for the rehabilitation of
rape victims exists in India. But the story of this only scheme
is even more ironic. In 1993, while hearing a case filed by
Delhi Domestic Working Women's Forum against the Union
of India and others, the Supreme Court of India had directed
the National Commission for Women (NCW) to evolve 'a
scheme so as to wipe out the tears of the unfortunate victims
of rape in India'. The NCW sent a rehabilitation scheme draft
to the central government in 1995. The draft lay as if in a
freezer for over a decade. Cut to 2005. The NCW finally came
up with a 'Scheme for Rehabilitation and Relief of Victims of
Rape, 2005'. The Commission proposed that the Ministry of
Home Affairs issue directives to all states governments for aid
to rape survivors, which includes shelter, legal help, vocational
training and proper long term rehabilitation.[13] After the

Delhi December gang-rape, women's rights activists in India again brought the issue of rehabilitation of rape victims to the forefront and demanded the implementation of the above said scheme. This made some fresh noise in public discourse. But neither the states nor central government had allocated a clear budget for this scheme. As proposed in the initial draft, National Mission for Empowerment of Women has the funds but no political will. Hidden away from the public glare in a most inaccessible manner, these issues command neither media nor political attention.[14]

A joint bench of Justices S.C. Dharmadhikari and S.B. Surkhe in Bombay High Court also came down heavily against the Maharashtra police while hearing a public interest litigation filed by the 'Forum against Oppression of Women' in July 2013. Ordering the directions for the constitution of a 'victim compensation fund' according to the above mentioned scheme, the judges famously said, 'Will you only register an FIR, investigate but not rehabilitate? There are children, minors (among the victims). Where will they go? The women and child development department does not have funds? Why are you not coming up with some mechanism and appropriate provision for helping rape victims? Where has your sensitivity gone?'[15]

But one reason behind the absence of proper laws regarding rehabilitation is that the Indian judiciary is still largely retributive in its mode of functioning and works on the principle of creating deterrents by punishing. Unlike developed countries like the United Kingdom and the United States of America, the Indian judiciary is still far away from developing a compensatory and rehabilitative justice model for itself.

## Retributive/deterrent model of justice versus compensatory and rehabilitative one

Traditionally, the victim has not received a prominent position in the criminal justice system as compared to the accused. As far as tracing the concept of compensation in victimology is concerned, the whole era till the mid-1900s can be generally divided into three parts. In the initial years of human civilization when humans started living together after the Stone Age, because of the absence of rule of law and authoritative political institution, the right to punish was with the individual. Hence, in a crude sense, the concept of compensation existed at that time. Then came the era in which social control in terms of mechanical solidarity creeped in and the offence against individuals lost its individualistic character. Instead, it became an offence against the tribe to which the individual belonged. Here the tribe replaced a victim's rights. The third stage was the advent of monarchy. So now, the king had the right to punish and would get monetary compensation.

Till the 1950s, this position largely remained as it is even after the advent of democracy. Then in the aftermath of the Second World War, the cause of victims finally got prominence when some radical criminologists championed the idea and established that criminology is also about the victims... not just the criminals.[16] In this context, American criminologists are referred to for saying the following in a book titled *New Horizons in Criminology* published in 1943: 'It is perhaps worth noting that our barbarian ancestors were wiser and more just than what we are today, for they adopted a theory of restitution to the injured, whereas we have abandoned this practice today, to the detriment of all concerned. Even where fines are imposed today, the state retains the proceeding and the victim gets no compensation.'[17]

In the Indian context, it is important to note that Article 21 of the Indian Constitution guarantees 'right to life' to all Indian citizens. This includes protection of life and liberty of all members of society. Also, the preamble of the Indian Constitution guarantees 'justice' to all Indian citizens. So, all victims of crime have a right to get justice and to remedy the harm suffered as a result of the crime. Also, right to access of justice and principle of fair trial mandates right of legal aid to the victims of crime. It also mandates protection to witnesses, counselling and medical aid to the victims and their bereaved families and in appropriate cases, rehabilitation measures including monetary compensation.[18] It is a paradox that a victim of a road accident gets this compensation under no fault theory but a victim of rape does not receive any compensation, barring a few exceptions in which final convictions take place.

Calling out for legal changes in the legislature to make it more sensitive towards the victims of crime, Supreme Court judge Justice Krishna Ayyar said, 'It is a weakness of our jurisprudence that the victims of crime and the distress of the dependents of the prisoners, do not attract the attention of law. Indeed, victim reparation is still the vanishing point of our criminal law. This is a deficiency in the system which be rectified by law' (Rattan Singh versus State of Punjab AIR 1980 Supreme Court 84).

Modern approaches to the concept of victimology acknowledges that a rape victim has every right to be adequately compensated, rehabilitated and repaired irrespective of the identification and prosecution of the offenders. And that payment of such compensation should be done by the state.

～

Ragini's story is a classic example explaining what happens in the aftermath of rape in India. Her story also brings out the explicit redundancy of single on-paper scheme India has for its rape survivors. Rehabilitation of rape survivors is indeed a very important issue but we need to start from first treating rape victims—and for that matter, women at large—as equal human beings who are ought to be treated with equal respect and dignity. In a country where judges start their judgments by saying, 'No amount of money can restore the dignity and confidence of rape victims' and that we need a rehabilitation scheme to 'wipe off the tears of the unfortunate rape victims', we clearly have a long way to go. By giving such statements judges not only reinforce the 'Oh, there is no life after rape' and 'You are what your body is' narrative, they also impose an unnecessary life-long burden of victimhood on a woman.

India is lagging far behind as far as rape rehabilitation polices are concerned. The only scheme available for the rehabilitation of rape victims itself appears to be a historical victim of bureaucratic lethargy, lack of political will and insensitive police departments. But, we have a far way to go, even to reach the point of 'rehabilitation of rape victim'.

In the Indian context, the idea of body chastity of women needs to be challenged. Until we dissociate the idea of 'pure and uncorrupted' body as central to a woman's existence, we will continue to make her life vulnerable by making her believe that if the crime of rape or sexual violence happens to her, it will be the end of her life. Fixing accountability, sensitizing police and medical practitioners in dealing with cases of sexual violence, efficient gathering of medical and circumstantial evidence, encouraging the victim to give her statement freely, ensuring a safe and fearless environment for the victim, medical aid, immediate monetary compensation and, later on, long term rehabilitation are other urgent steps which should be taken.

Justice is an important and grand idea. But it matters only if the idea of equality and dignity for women is implied in it.

Gender discrimination and violence against women are not going to end overnight in India. We have a long road ahead to travel—a road which will be full of conflicts, struggle, self doubts and also some occasional collateral damage. But, we must keep walking on this road. In search of a world where women feel safe and are treated as equal citizens; a world which is a fairer and a better place to live in for all human beings. But we must never forget that the starting point of this road is 'acknowledging' the insane amounts of violence happening against women all across the country, and beginning that process by listening. At the very least, we can start by believing in women.

# References

1. Albeena Shakil in her essay titled 'Rape and Honour Crime: The NCRB Report 2012' published in *The Economic and Political Weekly* on 3 August 2013. http://www.epw.in/journal/2013/31/web-exclusives/rape-and-honour-crimes-ncrb-report-2012.html.
2. Prachi Sharma, M.K. Unnikrinshnan and Abhishek Sharma in their article titled 'Sexual Violence in India: addressing gaps between policy and implementation' published in *Oxford Journals of Health Policy and Planning* on 6 February 2014.
3. Prachi Sharma, M.K. Unnikrinshnan and Abhishek Sharma in their article titled 'Sexual Violence in India: addressing gaps between policy and implementation' published in *Oxford Journals of Health Policy and Planning* on 6 February 2014.
4. Quoted from Kalpana Kannabiran's opinion piece published in *The Hindu* on 27 January 2013. http://www.thehindu.com/opinion/lead/a-moment-of-triumph-for-women/article4341113.ece.
5. Quoted from Albeena Shakil's article titled 'Protests, the Justice Verma Committee and the Government Ordinance' published in *The Economic and Political Weekly* on 9 February 2013. http://www.epw.in/journal/2013/06/web-exclusives/protests-justice-verma-committee-and-government-ordinance.html.
6. Quoted from a news story published in *The Hindu* on 3 February 2013. http://www.thehindu.com/news/national/ordinance-bypasses-all-vital-recommendations-of-verma-panel/article4372835.ece.
7. Quoted from Albeena Shakil's article titled 'Protests, the Justice

Verma Committee and the Government Ordinance' published in *The Economic and Political Weekly* on 9 February 2013. http://www.epw.in/journal/2013/06/web-exclusives/protests-justice-verma-committee-and-government-ordinance.html.

8. Reference taken from an editorial titled 'Misogyny Stalks Parliament' published in *The Economic and Political Weekly* on 30 March 2013. http://www.epw.in/journal/2013/13/editorials/misogyny-stalks-parliament.html.

9. Reference taken from a news item published on the United Nation's news centre website titled 'Opportunity lost, as new anti-rape laws in India fail to address root causes'. http://www.un.org/apps/news/story.asp?NewsID=44818#.Vt29SfmLSUl.

10. Quoted from a news item published in *The Hindu* titled 'Majority of rape cases go unreported' published in August 2013. http://www.thehindu.com/todays-paper/tp-national/tp-newdelhi/majority-of-rape-cases-go-unreported-mps/article5063089.ece.

11. Quoted from a news item published in *Deccan Herald* titled 'SC wants rehabilitation for rape victims' published on 5 August 2013. http://www.deccanherald.com/content/349364/sc-wants-rehabilitation-scheme-rape.html.

12. Quoted from an article titled 'The Trauma Never Ends' written by Vinita A. Shetty published in *India Together* news website on 2 September 2013. http://indiatogether.org/schemes-women.

13. Quoted from an article written by Neha Dixit titled 'How rape is only the beginning of a rape victim's nightmare' published in *DailyO* website on 18 November 2014. http://www.dailyo.in/politics/how-rape-is-only-the-beginning-of-a-victims-nightmare/story/1/849.html.

14. Quoted from an article written by Neha Dixit titled 'How rape is only the beginning of a rape victim's nightmare' published in *DailyO* website on 18 November 2014. http://www.dailyo.in/politics/how-rape-is-only-the-beginning-of-a-victims-nightmare/story/1/849.html.

15. Quoted from a news story titled 'High Court to State: Where is your sensitivity to victims of rape?' published in *The Times of India* on 23 July 2013. http://timesofindia.indiatimes.com/city/mumbai/

High-court-to-state-Where-is-your-sensitivity-to-victims-of-rape/
articleshow/21255602.cms?

16. Quoted from a research paper titled 'A critical study on the victims of rape: An analysis: The role of judiciary and government in their rehabilitation' written by Eakramuddin published in the *California Law Review* in 2014.

17. From the book *New Horizons in Criminology* published in 1943. https://books.google.co.uk/books/about/New_horizons_in_criminology.html?id=5cs1AAAAIAAJ&redir_esc=y.

18. From a research paper titled 'Compensation and Rehabilitation of Rape Survivors: A Constitutional Right' written by Mukesh Yadav, Pramendra Singh Thakur and Pooja Rastogi. Published in *Journal of Indian Academy and Forensic Medicine* in September 2014.

# Acknowledgements

To Nisha Susan—my magician, and to Gaurav Jain. The idea of doing this book germinated at the breakfast table of their home in August 2012.

To Dr Jitendra Suman—the first reader of all my first drafts during my first year as a reporter and writer. Also, for being my first window to literature, compassion and dreams.

To Brijesh Singh—my oldest friend on whose borrowed laptop I wrote this book; for his immeasurable affection and undying trust in me. And for always believing that I will finish this book one day.

Sanjay Dubey and Pawan K. Verma at the then *Tehelka Hindi* team—for trusting the reporter in me at a very young age.

Anant Nath, Vinod K. Jose, Ajay Krishnan and Roman Gautam at *The Caravan*.

The whole team behind *Grist Media*—for allowing me to do some of the most important stories of our times. Some of those stories are also part of this book.

In Bhopal—to Rakesh Dixit, Sravani Sarkar, P. Naveen and Shams Ur Rehman Alvi, Rubina Khan Shapoo, Rizwan Bhai and Pushpendra Pal Singh.

In the Northeast—to Ratnadeep Choudhary in Guwahati and Agnes Kharshiing in Shillong. Also, to the many people in Tripura who helped me on and off the field. They know who they are.

In Lucknow—to Himanshu Bajpai and to the city of Lucknow itself.

In Ranchi—to Nirala Bedesia for all the love and support.

In Delhi—to my Muneerka gang for all the love and laughter. Vikas Kumar, Suyash Bhai, Rashmi Ji and *didi*. To Imran Ali and Anant Asthana—for their friendship and support. To Anurag Vats and his beautiful library. And to Prashant Verma aka *Pehla Gorakhpuria*.

In London—to Anuradha Beniwal (Anu), my sunshine and pillar of strength.

In Bombay—to Renu Kashyap or *sunflower*, my soul-sister and the sky above my head. To Gaurav Solanki—my home and heart in Bombay.

To Ankita Kulshreshtha and Khushboo Joshi—always, my besties.

To Avijit Solanki and Sourabh Anant—for our mutual love of theatre, Bhopal and old friendships.

To Arshia Sattar, Rahul Soni at the beautiful Sangam House Writing Residency in Bangalore. I finished first drafts of three chapters during my time at Sangam in May 2015.

To the International Women's Media Foundation for selecting this book for The Howard G. Buffett Fund for Women Journalists. The money from this grant supported the reporting expenses of at least two chapters in this book.

I wrote the last chapter of this book during my time at the University of Westminster, London, where I went to study as a Chevening fellow—elected for the South Asia Journalism Program. I thank my professors Jean Seaton and Rosie Thomas at the university for encouraging me. Also, to Daisy Hasan, for always being there.

To Swami Vivekanand Library of Bhopal and its 'parent' Laxshmi Sharan Mishra—for being the ultimate game changer of my life.

To Parikshit Sharma and Mayur Dubey—for growing up with me.

To Rahul Pandita—one of my own.

To Gagan Gill and Nirmal Verma.

To all the sources, local reporters, lawyers and activists—who not only went out their way in helping me while doing the stories in difficult circumstances, but also always opened their hearts and homes for me.

To Dharini Bhaskar—this book belongs to you.

To Himanjali Sankar—thank you for making this book what it is.

To Sayantan Ghosh—thank you for always having my back.

For Rahul and Bharti—driving forces behind this book.

To Pran Nath and Rajni Dhar—for accepting me as I am. And for giving me immeasurable love and a home.

To Mamta Bua—for always being by my side.

To Rishabh and Nishant—my younger brothers, my children.

To Dr King Jee Dhar—for home, peace and love.

To Sita and Awadhesh Dubey—my beloved parents, for everything.

To all the survivors and their families, who, over the years, shared their stories with me.

And to Bhopal, my beloved city: *mera mehboob shehar.*